Educational Policy and Social Reproduction

This book takes a theoretically informed look at British education policy over the last 60 years when secondary schooling for all children became an established fact for the first time. Comprehensive schools largely replaced a system based on academic selection. Now, under choice and competition policies, all schools are subject to the rigours of local education markets. What impact did each of these successive policy frameworks have on structures of opportunities for families and their children? How and to what extent was the experience of secondary school students shaped and what influenced the qualifications they obtained and their life chances after schooling?

The authors locate their work within two broad strands in the sociology of education. Basil Bernstein's work on the realisation of power and control in and through pedagogic discourse and social reproduction provides a theoretical framework for exploring the character of, and continuities and change in, education and training policies.

This book is an important contribution to debates about the extent to which education is a force for change in class-divided societies. The authors also set out to re-establish social class at the centre of educational analysis at a time when emphasis has been on identity and identity formation, arguing for their interdependence. This book will be an important resource for students, policy analysts and policy-makers wishing to think through and understand the longer term impact of programmes that have shaped secondary schooling in Britain and elsewhere.

John Fitz is Professor of Education in the School of Social Sciences, Cardiff University, Wales. **Brian Davies** is Professor of Education in the School of Social Sciences, Cardiff University, Wales. **John Evans** is Professor of Sociology of Education and Physical Education at Loughborough University, England.

Educational Policy and Social Reproduction

Class inscription and symbolic control

John Fitz, Brian Davies and John Evans

Routledge
Taylor & Francis Group

LONDON AND NEW YORK

First published 2006
by Routledge
2 Park Square, Milton Park, Abingdon, Oxon OX14 4RN

Simultaneously published in the USA and Canada
by Routledge
270 Madison Ave, New York, NY 10016

Routledge is an imprint of the Taylor & Francis Group

© 2006 John Fitz, Brian Davies and John Evans

Typeset in Bembo by
HWA Text and Data Management, Tunbridge Wells
Printed and bound in Great Britain by
TJ International Ltd, Padstow, Cornwall

British Library Cataloguing in Publication Data
A catalogue record for this book is available from the British Library

Library of Congress Cataloging in Publication Data
A catalog record for this book has been requested

ISBN 0–415–24004–2 (hbk)
ISBN 0–415–24005–0 (pbk)

Contents

Illustrations

Diagrams

Figures

Tables

Abbreviations

CACE	Central Advisory Council for Education
CASE	Campaign for the Advancement of State Education
CATE	Council for the Accreditation of Teacher Education
CEP	Centre for Economic Performance
CTC	City Technology Colleges
DES	Department of Education and Science
DfES	Department for Education and Skills
EAZ	Education Action Zone
EDP	Education Development Plan
ERA	Education Reform Act
FSM	free school meals
GPSDT	Girls' Public School Day Trust
GM	grant-maintained
HHR	Halsey, Heath and Ridge
HMI	Her Majesty's Inspectorate
HE	higher education
IPPR	Institute of Public Policy Research
KS	Key Stage
LEA	local education authority
LMS	local management of schools
LSE	London School of Economics
MSC	Manpower Services Commission
NCDS	National Child Development Study
NCVQ	National Council for Vocational Qualifications
NC	National Curriculum
NFER	National Foundation for Educational Research
NVQ	National Vocational Qualification
OFSTED	Office for Standards in Education
PFI	private finance initiative
QCA	Qualifications and Curriculum Authority
SMTs	senior management teams
SENCO	special educational needs coordinator
TGAT	Task Group on Assessment and Testing

TTA	Teaching Training Agency
TVEI	Technical and Vocational Education Initiative
TPS	totally pedagogised society
TA	Training Agency
YTS	youth training scheme
VA	voluntary aided
WAG	Welsh Assembly Government

1 Understanding policy, understanding pedagogic discourse

Introduction

Policy studies come in all shapes and sizes. This one arises from our collective experience of being teachers and researchers in British schools and universities over the past 40 years, along the way becoming sociologists under the influence of Basil Bernstein at the Institute of Education, University of London in the 1960s and 1970s. We confess as much upfront because the initial experience was seminal and the influence lasting. It gave us the deepest respect for a number of notions that: theory without research was nothing and vice versa; the 'isms' of social science were places where people banded together for company, as much as sources of warmth as light; and that who and what we were emerged from the labyrinthine interactions of class and identity. We were what we knew, how we said it, how we recognised, responded to and exercised knowledge and control. Our common experience was of rising through education and we were passionate about its inequalities.

In recent years we have taught about policy at undergraduate, Masters' and doctoral levels and researched it in contexts ranging from ability grouping, vocational initiatives, inspection, national testing and changing aspects of diversity and choice in secondary schools, to including PE in the National Curriculum, small and medium enterprise linkage with education and training in Wales and Germany, changing the nursing curriculum and eating disorders. We have lived through the period since 1944 that we make the focus of this book with an increasing urge to understand what part policy making and makers have had in shaping it.

While we have set out to produce a text that is accessible to undergraduates, postgraduates and practitioners this is not a textbook in the sense of setting out to be deliberately compendious. We will attempt to locate what we offer (and do not) in a brief depiction of what studies of educational policy conventionally range over before elaborating the themes that we intend to explore. First, we want to remind you that education is not the only field of policy studies and that looking at the best work in others, such as health and housing is extremely worthwhile and can throw all sorts of light on controversies in our field. Second, those of you who are already familiar with policy analyses will need no reminding and those of you who are not deserve warning that this is a field characterised by many approaches and vocabularies. All of the social sciences, like economics, sociology and psychology and their hybrids, such as politics and management, as well as disciplines like history, law and philosophy have valid contributions to make to policy studies. Many of these contributions are not easily reconciled, let alone synthesised. Third, there is the question of what we are referring to when we talk of 'policy'. The term is used in all sorts of ways, for example to refer to everyday behaviour where, of course, honesty continues to be generally the best policy, the deliberated behaviour of business organisations to give us what we want at a profit and the activity of the state and its various agencies in determining what will be provided through the public sector, from defence to welfare. We are concerned with the latter with particular respect of education. But we are conscious that it is a long way from Ministers, civil servants, advisers, lobbyists and legislatures in central government to the sites where teachers and students do the things (or not) that policymakers appear to require of them and that the loop that connects them (or not) goes through a number of state-created other agencies, as well as the 'local state'. Indeed, in federal systems, like the USA, the latter is directly responsible for education while in unitary states, like Britain, a changing balance of responsibility has been shared between central state and local authorities, mainly counties. The 'machinery' of government through which education policy and provision is framed and delivered everywhere differs (even between the parts of Britain – England, Wales, Scotland and Northern Ireland) and has changed over time.

While this sets us all the task of grasping the terminologies and institutional practices of any given system (try, for example, the British 'White Paper', a discussion document published by government in advance of intended legislation that outlines its likely content, or US Supreme Court judgements, that arise out of conflict and litigation over specific events and generally constrain state practices) they remain mere mechanics without a sense of their histories and the dynamics of the power and control hierarchies that they represent. Such problems and choices that arise in acquiring insight on the nature of policy studies are reflected in the emphases found in the literature, not least in sociological analyses of educational policy. Approaching them in Goldilocks' spirit of gastronomy can be useful. For some tastes and purposes some are too global or too national or too local; others insufficiently detailed, some immured in technical detail; many lose individual actors in the structural wood and vice versa; and 'bricolage' is everywhere, turning explanation of the apparent randomness of some policy processes into 'flailing around for anything that looks as if it might work' (Ball, 1998: 126). Everyone who wishes to avoid being mistaken for an officially sponsored jobber adopts the label 'critical'. It is well to recognise at the outset that there is no 'just nice', no definitive account of educational policy and its effects, there are more or less adequate ones from some perspectives, for given purposes. While lots of honest, rational endeavour is poured in to policy making it would be a mistake to picture it simply as the domain of wise people seeking clear and just goals. Partiality, ideology and self-seeking are mixed with altruism and pursuit of 'public interest'. Moreover, there is a rich and dynamic interior to processes and the sites where they take place. Many ideologically accented voices clamour for attention to their own causes. Institutions, whether departments of state, 'think tanks', official agencies, publishers, teachers' associations, local education committees or school staffrooms all have 'lives of their own'. To borrow Lee Shulman's marvellous observation on classrooms, 'stuff happens', everywhere there is play and contingency at the lived end of the forces of power and control. As Evans' account of making the national curriculum in PE makes clear, even the most carefully picked teams evolve their own game plan (Evans, 1990; Penney and Evans, 1999)

We make two suggestions, the first in the spirit of improving discrimination of different styles of work, based on the 'general observations' made by Taylor *et al.* (1997: 14–17) about the scope and complexity of educational policy which structure their book. For them, policy making is a multidimensional and value-laden state activity that exists in context. Policy is always more than the text and in education it interacts with those in other fields. Their 'implementation' is never straightforward and they 'result in unintended as well as intended consequences'. While we share their view that the 'policy sciences' were long dominated by rational and technicist 'best way' approaches we do not accept their root and branch castigation of 'the positivist assumption that social scientific knowledge can be value-neutral'. Real worries and reservations about objectivity in social science are not to be mended by its complete rejection and finding the problems or pretensions of encompassing theories or 'modernism' difficult is not solved, for us, by leaps into relativism or postmodernist turns. To believe that well theorised empirical work can lead to reliable knowledge is not to abandon being 'critical' or to become 'underlabourers' to the powerful who tend to initiate policy.

Our second suggestion follows, we hope understandably, from taking this position and it is to look, above all, for a way of conceptualising policy origins, processes and destinations sociologically that allows us to stay in touch with the insightful view of Taylor *et al.* of their complexity and scope while also retaining the view that appropriate languages of description are possible that connect empirical and theoretical work. We believe that this no more precludes holding strong and critical views of social arrangements and processes than it guarantees to shape the behaviour of the powerful in directions of which we would approve. We would suggest that one exists in terms of Basil Bernstein's ideas formed over almost fifty years of writing and researching pedagogic relations in families and schools in interaction with others whose active work on them continues. We will briefly delineate them in the next section, having first attempted to show what wider aspects of our concerns that they attend to.

Bernstein's sociology: a language for policy

In the first place, we recognise having lived through a lifetime of what might be called the internecine sociological wars Bernstein's (1975: Chapter 7; 1999) long standing concern with the character of sociological knowledge led him to argue that it belonged to the category of horizontal knowledge structures – flat, segmented, non-cumulative and weakly theorised – in strong contrast to vertical structures, such as physics that were strongly hierarchical, theoretical and strove to unity. He characterised sociologists, not least in education, as being concerned with 'commitment to a language' rather than 'dedication to a problem and its vicissitudes'. The 'array of specialist languages' that we rather tacitly acquired, whose diversity allows us to image 'the potential of the social in its different modes of realisation' stood in need of 'challenge by the dynamic interactional process of research', not so much displaced as repositioned (Bernstein, 1999: 170).

The concepts with which he worked were shaped by a wide range of others, though predominantly Durkheimian (Davies, 1994; Muller, 2000) and always stood in intimate and open relation with work in progress or its possibility. They are an important antidote both to 'isms' that exclude others and that substitute commitment for testing. In the first instance they derived from what for most individuals would have been a lifetime of sociolinguistic work on the concept of 'code' and the reproduction of class relationships 'as they shaped the structure of communication, and its social basis in the family'. From the 1970s they shifted in focus to analyses of schools 'against a broader canvas of changes in forms of social control' without losing sight on the analysis of 'the grim consequences of class relationships' (Bernstein, 1975: 1). By 1996 (p. 12) he represented this work as having been empirically mainly about 'class inscription' and theoretically 'increasingly concerned with general questions of pedagogic communication as a crucial medium of symbolic control' and prospectively about 'understanding the social processes whereby consciousness and desire are given specific forms, evaluated, distributed, challenged and changed'. In such quests 'policy' takes its place as one mode of attempting control of the 'pedagogic device' and we have a framework that encompasses it.

The term 'pedagogic device' is one that readers often find most puzzling in Bernstein until realising that, like all else in his analysis of education, it stands in direct line to his earlier sociolinguistic work. In linguistics the term 'language device' is used, not without controversy, to refer to a system of formal rules that governs the combinations made when we speak or write, in Chomskyan terms based on two facilities, a built-in sensitivity to their acquisition and an inter-actional one that makes acquisition possible. For him, its rules, acquisition and possibilities are stable and independent of culture. For Bernstein (1996: 41) and Halliday (1978), the rules of the language device, the 'carrier' of our language relays, while stable, 'may well have their origin in the concerns of dominant groups' so that they are not neutral, have 'some very fundamental classifications, in particular gender classifications' built in. What is 'carried' or relayed relies on contextual rules that depend, for example, on whether we are talking to teacher or soulmate. The pedagogic device is similar, like the language device having internal rules which regulate the pedagogic communication that it makes possible, acting selectively on potential pedagogic meanings. Its forms of realisation also vary with context and, while also stable, are not ideologically free. Both provide rulers for consciousness.

Viewed metaphorically 'the pedagogic device provides the intrinsic grammar of pedagogic discourse' (ibid.: 42) through its inter-related distributive, recontextualising and evaluative rules. Distributive rules specialise forms of knowledge, consciousness and practice to social groups and govern the changing line between the esoteric and the mundane. 'Power relations distribute the thinkable and the unthinkable' and regulate the possibilities of alternative order and society while they 'differentiate and stratify groups accomplished by the distributive rules' (ibid.: 45). They also create a specialised field of production of discourse, the rules of entry to and control of which are more and more controlled by the state itself. Recontextualising rules, derived from them, constitute specific pedagogic discourses which always embed instructional rules, which create skills of one kind or another and specify their relationship, in regulative discourse, rules that create social order, relations and identity. Though often researched separately as competence and values they are one and delocate other discourses, like physics or history and recontextualise them as school subjects. The recontextualising field has both official (made up of the state and its selected agents and ministries, the ORF) and pedagogic (including, among others, individuals in school and colleges, teacher educators, private research enterprise, journals and textbook publishers, the PRF) actors. The extent of the scope allowed to pedagogic recontextualisers is the measure of education's autonomy, by no means guaranteed and which, in recent decades, has been shrunk by the greater incursion of governments generally invoking arguments, as if the relationship was one way, about schools' inability to deliver an adequate service to their increasingly globalised economies. Both cooperation and conflict of greater or lesser intensity exists between official and pedagogic agents over exerting influence over all aspects of educational arrangements and practices, not least the rules of order of school subjects concerning content selection, relation, sequence and pace (the expected rate of acquisition), as well as the theory of instruction and its model of the learner.

Bernstein insisted that both these 'what' and 'how' aspects of pedagogic discourse contained ideological elements and were 'never wholly utilitarian' (p. 47). Finally, pedagogic discourse which specialises time, text and space and brings them into special relation, is transformed into pedagogic practice. Time is transformed into arbitrary age categories, text into content and space into specific context. Age is then, in turn, transformed into acquisition, text into evaluation and context into transmission. It is continuous evaluation that is 'the key to pedagogic practice', condensing the meaning of the whole pedagogic device. From the classroom nod-and-wink to the formal examination, evaluation is involved in the reproduction by 'teachers' of chosen content or text that has originated with knowledge producers and has been recontextualised, turned into its 'imaginary' school version, by specialised state and educational agencies for transmission to 'acquirers' categorised in particular ways, particularly age, stage and, sometimes, gender. Our experiences of these specialisations of 'text, time and and space marks us cognitively, socially and culturally' (pp. 49–50). Nothing is neutral, everything is weighed and valued.

While such ideas appear very general in character they are, in fact, condensations of what we know happens across educational systems and suggest that educational, like language devices, will be essentially the same everywhere. A good deal of the early research that went in to such ideas was carried out by Bernstein's students in education systems, such as those of Portugal and Chile (see particularly, Bernstein, 1996: Chapter 5) and, indeed, there are aspects of systems, across time and societies that show remarkable durability and little variation. Comparative educators, the shell-collectors of the subject everywhere, have made a very good living at laying them out. But this is to miss the point. While everywhere is the same it is also different, as borrowing and attempting to transplant bits of systems, historically mainly one of the perils of underdevelopment, largely attests by regularly 'failing' or ending up appreciably differently. Such failure usually resides in not recognising the primacy of regulative discourse over instructional. Good recent examples would be the attempt to import primary school practices from a country like Taiwan into English classrooms in initiatives, such as the Literacy and Numeracy Hours (Alexander, 1996) or English competence pedagogy into Palestinian primaries (Al-Ramahi and Davies, 2002). Educational identities, the production of one sort or another of which is the object of all pedagogic discourse and practice, differ in distinctive cultural and market conditions. They are the product of complex ensembles of arrangements and resources that Bernstein (1971) initially suggested could be typologised as collection and integrated codes marked, respectively, by strong and weak classification of knowledge boundaries and framing (mainly control over pacing) of contents. The first tended to be characterised by visible and explicit rules. The latter by more hidden and tacit ones. Bernstein later (1996) refined these into a notion of two main models of pedagogic practice, performance and competence, distinguished by time, space and discourse (whether content was presented as subjects or themes), evaluation, control, pedagogic text (whether the learner's output or what teacher sees it as signifying), autonomy and economy. 'Performance' might be taken as the dominant, established model, a comet with a very long historical tail, with specialisation of clearly marked subjects, skills and procedures, explicit recognition and realisation rules for legitimate texts and strong stratification between students. Space and movement were likely to be strongly marked. With the focus upon acquirers' past and future accomplishments, with strong, apparent progression and pacing, evaluation focused on what was missing from their texts in terms of explicit and specific criteria of which they were made aware. Their texts were products of their performance, to be graded and repair systems made available to those who did not meet them. Order was strongly relayed through explicit positional control.

In contrast, within a competence mode, whose origin he traced to 'a remarkable convergence' in the 1960s in the social sciences around its 'social logic' (Bernstein, 1996: 55), content was presented in terms of themes, projects and ranges of experience with a group base and acquirers had a measure of control over selection, sequence and pace. Space tended to be constructed and current states emphasised, weak sequencing, lack of apparent progression and implicit pacing rules throwing emphasis on what acquirers were currently revealing. Evaluation focus was on acquirers' texts by the transmitter/facilitator and control tended to the personal rather than positional, focusing upon intentions, dispositions, relations and reflexivity. The text indicated acquirers' cognitive and social development. Teachers and students needed a range of autonomy, more so than in most performance modes, which were also generally less expensive, more subject to the economies of external control. They were less time-consuming than the demands of resource construction, individualising profiling and pacing and teacher liaison, among other things, in performance modes.

Competence modes, while all focusing on 'procedural commonalities shared within a group' (p. 63) could be further distinguished as: liberal/progressive which saw 'similar to' relations located within the individual, 'intra-individual potential that could be revealed by appropriate pedagogic practice' (p. 64), legitimising child development and professional careers for women, sponsored by a new middle class located in the field of symbolic control; a populist mode, locating 'similar to' relations or indigenous competences within a local class, ethnic or regional culture felt to be dominated or ignored; and what might be called the 'Freireian' mode that also located competence within a local, dominated group to be unlocked by exploring the source of their own powerlessness through appropriate pedagogy. While the first has become part of official and pedagogic recontexualising fields, and the second is cautiously recognised as part of a revivification of the 'locality' in a world structured by increasingly global processes (Castells, 1997), the third may only inhabit the fringes of the latter.

Bernstein's claim was that differing performance modes, all based on 'different to' relations, 'are empirically normal across all levels of official education', whereas competence modes 'may be seen as interrupts or resistances to this normality or may be appropriated by official education for specific and local purposes', 'generally found regulating the early life of acquirers or in repair sections' (p. 65). It is particularly important, then, that we grasp the character of these performance modes and the identities that they seek to engender that will have been the focus of struggle for shape and control by policymakers and classroom practitioners alike. Bernstein distinguished three modes in terms of their knowledge base, focus and social organisation, singulars, regions and generic. School discourse has been firmly based on singulars, knowledge structures with unique names, specialised, discrete discourses with their own texts and practices, rules of entry, examinations and licenses to practise. They are generally narcissistic, protected by strong boundaries and hierarchies, they are physics, chemistry, history, etc., the disciplines that figure in the school curriculum. They come and go only at its margins. Regions recontextualise singulars 'into larger units which operate both in the intellectual field of the disciplines and in the field of external practice' (p. 65). Some are well-established and long-standing, like engineering, medicine and architecture, others newer, like cognitive science or communications and media, having grown at pace in higher education as it has expanded and diversified. New singulars may enter regions, as in sociology to medicine, depending on their recontextualising principle and social base. Open to greater central administrative control and oriented outward to markets, regions tend to weaken the discursive and political base of disciplines.

Regionalisation signals a change from narcissistic, subject-based, introjected identities to more externally dependent, projected ones. Schools have resisted or rejected it very well, though. However, they have come under some pressure to move to the generic, as in Britain when Conservative governments in the 1980s became, at least in part, persuaded by the arguments of their 'industrial trainer' (Ball, 1990) supporters. They called for changes that would enable young people to be better equipped to meet 'the needs of industry'. Combined with the existence of unprecedented levels of youth unemployment, brought about by industry and government inability to control change and recession in labour markets but ideologically transformed into the responsibility of a 'failing' school system, such appeals persuaded policy makers that appropriate change and response could only be achieved by moving altogether outside the influence of the existing agents of the official and pedagogic recontextualising fields.

Their locus shifted to the Department of Employment and its Manpower Services Commission (MSC) which devised the school and college based work oriented Technical Vocational Educational Initiative (TVEI) which schools rapidly subverted and turned to their performance oriented ends (see Chapter 6). It had more success through its Training Agency (TA) which, in association with the Youth Training Scheme (YTS), developed a 'competence' methodology that underpinned the awards of the National Council for Vocational Qualifications (NCVQ). This focused essentially on work and 'life' and rapidly transformed the Further Education sector, expunging liberal education and craft traditions, privileging functional analyses of 'competences' that were taken to be necessary features of performing skills or tasks and giving 'rise to a jejune concept of trainability' (Bernstein, 1996: 67). NCVQ pedagogic and assessment modes have also gained a foothold in British schools, mainly as alternative post-compulsory routes for students regarded as unsuited to or unwilling in the face of subject modes. Though generic modes rest on the 'similar to' principle that characterises those of competence modes, they point to projected identities, for it is general skills underlying specific performances that constitute the similarity.

In a world where 'flexible' labour rather than long-term jobs or careers are deemed normal, its underlying principle is 'trainability' where individuals are regarded as having 'something' crucial to their own and the economy's survival residing in 'the ability to respond effectively to concurrent, subsequent, intermittent pedagogies', capable of being 'formed and reformed according to technological, organisational and market contingencies'. But, in Bernstein's view, 'to respond to such a future depends upon a capacity, not an ability' that relies upon a preceding, specialised identity. The response must be on the basis of something other than individual psychological boot-strapping, so that the concept of trainability is socially empty and identities shift toward the 'materialities of consumption' (p. 73). The prospect of extension of generic modes is taken up in

Chapter 6. As is widely argued in the literature, postmodern or networked societies are ones where traditionally ascribed categories, such as age, gender and age relations have become weakened as collective bases of stable, unambiguous identities, as have the class and occupational ones that we achieve, creating new possibilities in their construction. A state newly active in such construction work is as likely to get the job out of kilter with what its 'clients', families and students and 'shareholders' (businesses, if the rhetoric is to be believed) want and expect as it is in any other of its undertakings, expending a good deal of specialised resource along the way.

Bernstein suggested that combinations of demographic, social, economic and knowledge change underlaid events in Britain over the period to which we refer when official and pedagogic recontextualising fields permitted or engendered change from performance to competence modes and somewhat back again. The state exercised no direct control, as we shall see, over pedagogic contents or modes of transmission for a considerable period after the 1944 Education Act. The changed arrangements that flowed from it altered practice little. In the ugly phrase of the time, the new, unselective ('modern') secondary schools 'aped' the grammars, the highly prized, socially elite, known world, while primaries struggled for identities beyond the 'standards' or grades in terms of which they had long invited children to perform.

By the 1960s, particularly exercised through their control of teacher training, pedagogic recontextualisers were widely convinced of the emancipatory potential of liberal-progressive competence modes, particularly for the new primary schools. Various degrees of 'child centredness' became institutionalised, puzzling and delighting parents and their children in different degrees. It was believed to be particularly beneficial for the 'have nots', while proceeding from the social basis of the 'haves', a source of some contradiction. At the secondary level, again as we shall see, the 'comprehensivisation' that was becoming increasingly usual constituted a change in organisational form only. Permitted by a rather reluctant central state, however, it 'created an autonomous local space for the construction of curriculum and the manner of its acquisition' through the removal of some or all overt selection. While sociology of education's contribution to such issues amounted to little more than the blindest of gropes up a dead-end alley labelled 'New Directions' (Young, 1971), where all knowledge promised to be equal, more than a few teachers and schools individually innovated more successfully in search of better solutions to the poor fit of singular modes to the plurality of their students. In a period up to the mid-1970s of full employment, relatively high juvenile wages, changing youth cultures and, in some areas, changing ethnic identity, attitudes and responses to schools' regulative discourse, as to other forms of authority, became more conditional. It also marked the end of what was to prove 'a unique set of conditions' of 'autonomy of the PRF and ideological rapport between that field and the ORF' (Bernstein, 1996: 72).

The period that followed from the late 1970s saw a considerable reversal of these trends, as we will show in Chapters 7 and 8. School survival and growth came to depend increasingly 'upon optimising a market niche, upon objective productions, upon value-adding procedures' (ibid.). Local Education Authorities' (LEAs) responsibilities were largely removed, agents in the PRF repositioned, removed or ignored and a period of increasingly direct official state intervention though a range of new, directly appointed agencies began. Schools, colleges and universities entered the age of 'performativity' (Ball, 2000), relatively more isolated and self-scanning in the pursuit of others' targets that they were required to make their own. Newly entrepreneurial school managements had to compete in a time-consuming bidding culture, where improvement initiatives offering resources to 'those who can' have replaced allocation to 'those that ought to', from which only the elite are exempt. Middle-class parents in Britain and elsewhere were perceived to get angry with 'equity reforms', with politicians eyeing, in the words of Michael Barber, Head of the UK School Standards and Effectiveness Unit, an 'impatient electorate' restless with, among other things, what Prime Minister Blair had called 'bog standard comprehensive schools' (both quoted in Ball, 2003: 38).

Class conditions, demands and interests lie at the centre of educational policy. In the original edition of his last book, Bernstein attempted to lay out the conditions for an effective democracy and to measure education against the model of rights (to enhancement, inclusion and participation, at individual, social and political levels) that he thought were entailed. He condensed his claim, made initially in 1970 at the British Sociological Association's annual conference, that '(H)ow a society selects, classifies, distributes, transmits and evaluates the educational knowledge it considers to be public, reflects both the distribution of power and the principles of social control' (Bernstein, 1975: 85), to the metaphor of the school holding up a mirror in which was reflected a hierarchy of class values. Some images were negative, some positive, some excluded. Different knowledges, carrying unequal value, power and potential, were differentially distributed to social groups, greater resources going to the most prestigious, as also occurred with respect of other public and private goods and services outside the school system. Moreover, school types were and are not equivalent and pre-school provision, along with access to other social goods, skew it in favour of 'haves'.

Teachers sensitive to the possibilities and contribution of all their pupils, operating in a context which provided 'the conditions for effective acquisition, and an education which enables reflection on what is to be acquired and how it is to be acquired' (Bernstein, 1996: 8), notwithstanding the skill and success of some in inauspicious circumstances, were more likely to be found in 'better' schools. Schools have to deal with how external hierarchies and those which exist within themselves are reconciled and appear justified. They do so in two ways, first by appearing neutral, claiming to treat all students and families alike, while differentiating individuals and groups in terms of attainment. Some families and students, of course, know very well that they are not treated neutrally. Second, they create a discourse that emphasises group communality, generally horizontal solidarities, among staff and students through a mythical discourse that celebrates a common national consciousness and by attempting to disconnect their stratification system from that outside.

The curriculum and school rituals have always been sites for sustaining and reworking national consciousness which incorporates the equivalence, despite differences in power and opportunity, of the values and contributions of differing classes, genders, religions, ethnic and other social categories and groups. Single sex education has largely disappeared, multiculturalism recoils in the face of affirmative action, Christian religion, notwithstanding its continuing, compulsory character, has now become a cipher in most state schools that are not explicitly parochial in character. Schools' great organising principle is age, the neutral solidarity of the year group becoming the basis for the potentially highly divisive business of ability differentiation. Inequalities are legitimised by individuating failure, as the responsibility of the family and its endowment to the child, rather than implicating teachers or their teaching in general, though official discourse now distinguishes between the effective and ineffective while disallowing any consideration of their linkage to the system's organisational structures.

We take then, as our text, Bernstein's judgement that '(E)ducation preserves structural relations between social groups but changes structural relations between individuals and the latter is sufficient to create the impression of general and probable movement' (ibid.: 11). Patterns of educational success and failure have long been, and continue to be, strongly influenced by class which, in turn, mediates patterns by gender and ethnicity. It may seem paradoxical, therefore, that class has substantially disappeared from sociological discourse about educational policy. There have been, of course, real and substantial upward, overall shifts in affluence and living standards in Britain and most other societies outside the third world over the past 60 years. By the 1960s the 'affluent worker' debate in Britain swung around the contention that 'we are all middle class now'. While we never were and still are not, conditions and consciousnesses have changed. Class distribution has altered continuously, as measured by a variety of means centring round occupational hierarchy. This has been reflected in changing attempts to measure it, long dominated by the official Registrar General's socio-economic ratings, from the 1920s onwards ranging from professional and managerial, through clerical and supervisory, to skilled, semi- and unskilled working class, often collapsed to I, II and III.

Later computations, mainly originating in the Oxford Mobility Studies (Halsey *et al.*, 1980; Goldthorpe *et al.*, 1980) have attempted to take into account working-class skill shifts and shrinkage, as well as growth and diversification of middle-range and middle-class occupations, particularly incorporating ownership and the scope and degree of responsibility and introducing new terms, such as service class and salariat and dealing more adequately with categories of unemployment and exclusion, though still focusing essentially on male mobility (see Evans and Davies, 2005).

Better lives in better housing, with improved health and schools, more jobs and new and more plentiful goods and services in a burgeoning welfare state under a postwar Labour, then Conservative governments of the 1950s, shifted the policy balance toward the social market and the overt interests of labour rather than capital. Global technological and market trends were, though, even more rapidly internationalising capital and, in an era referred to as 'post-Fordism' (Burrows and Loader, 1994), led to concerted policy change to hasten a repositioning of these interests, in a 1970s of oil-shock and growing unemployment. Conservative Prime Minister Macmillan's celebratory claim in the late 1950s that we 'had never had it so good' became Thatcher's assertion in the 1980s that there is no such thing as society, only the family and individuals, the implications of which for educational policy, as we shall see, are, with only marginal modification, very much with us today.

Economists have long extolled the virtues of the 'trickle down effect' where competitive forces are allowed to increase the total volume of wealth, without concern about distributional consequences that tend to follow in terms of the increasing share of the already wealthy, so that benefits might reach down to those least advantaged and all will have risen in consequence. While this has been a view carrying undoubted meaning for upper, middle and affluent working-class families who may recognise themselves more in terms of their consumption status and possibilities (Cahill, 1994), it has been cold comfort to groups left out by policy processes which have, at times, seen unemployment as necessary to economic discipline and privatisation and outsourcing as handmaidens of inherently more efficient production outside the public section. We have produced a benefit-dependent underclass that is paralleled by our educational 'have nots'. In the tempting rhetoric of elements of the media, scrupulously courted by policy makers, the former tend to be depicted as scroungers, the latter misbehavers, neither working and both as objects of fear and blame.

None of these phenomena are particularly British. The problems of economic and social inequality, unemployment and social inclusion are endemic to societies of all types. What differs is their resource and inclination to define and deal with them. In education, symptomatically, the vocabularies for identifying them are those of 'under achievement' and 'inappropriate skill formation'. These, like drop-out and truancy, are very largely class phenomena, though officially they are never talked about in this way. In fact, class as a category and as a feature of sociological analysis was subject to something of an eclipse as the post-modern shadow of doubt over the legitimacy of such terms left us in Parisian gloom. The privileging of the subjectivity and relativism of discourses that post-modernism was taken to indicate experienced little resistance in much of the sociology of education and is still *à la mode* for many. But discourse is not all unless it makes explicit relationships between symbolic and social structures. Power may well be everywhere and constitutive but its distribution differs, with real consequences.

This initial period of doubt about our trade roughly coincided with (or maybe it helped some to rationalise) Conservative policy makers coming to a considered view that sociologists had very little light to shed on what they were interested in, as well as their determination to accelerate substantial change in teacher education the acknowledged stronghold in the PRF of the advocacy of competence modes. It was to be taken away from the disciplines of education, such as philosophy, history and sociology and towards school subjects and their delivery, backed by compliant readings from developmental and cognitive psychology. The school experience of teacher education staff, was from the 1980s on, to become substantially more 'recent and relevant' to current school practice. Sociologists of education became a diaspora sheltering in curricular, multicultural and policy studies, whose parapets stood slightly higher. Bernstein was not one of them but his sociology enables us to understand their work all the better.

On our omissions

Finally, we turn to the issue of the shape of the rest of this book. In a volume of this size it seemed evident to us that we could only do justice to a relatively narrow selection of policy issues. Our key focus is on the last 60 years' events, since the landmark Education Act, 1944, in relation to class reproduction and schooling, particularly in England and Wales. We are acutely conscious that there are many omissions and gaps. For example, we lack, apart from passing reference, a comparative or cross-cultural dimension. What has happened in Britain over the past 60 years, and particularly in the last 30 years, has strong resonances with what has occurred elsewhere, not only in historically directly connected other systems, such as Australia, New Zealand and South Africa but in much of Europe and North America. In the USA systemic school reform is almost as varied as its state and school district systems, although Chicago economics hovers nearly everywhere.

The politics of diversity and choice (see Chapters 7 and 8) has bitten hard in societies as far apart as New Zealand and the Netherlands, even if social market Scandinavia, centralised France and traditionalist Italy and Greece, for example, appear to remain largely immune. The UAE and Malaysia seek to move from didacticism to more student-autonomous systems. Taiwan, with over 100 per cent availability of higher education places, smiles politely at the news that we are seeking to emulate its allegedly high inference questioning, whole class primary teaching techniques and bases its reform on an image of British child-centredness. We live very much in a self-conscious, size matters with respect to student achievement, emulatory, policy borrowing, educational world. We know that we would have a different and, in some ways, better book if we had the space to weave in these experiences. We are aware of and value them and their stories would only confirm, by and large, our argument about the centrality of class.

We also fail to deal with gender and ethnicity, the other crucial categories that Bernstein insisted marked educational experience and realise that we lay ourselves open to considerable opprobrium in so doing. We are not denying their importance, for neither patriarchy nor prejudice/discrimination are simply reducible to class and merit the fullest consideration in their own right which, again, space does not permit. We recognise that if the great achievement of education in our time is massive overall increase in outputs and achievement in terms of public examinations and higher educational entry, then the transformation of those of girls and women is even more remarkable, by the same criteria and deserves much more attention than being treated as an epiphenomenon, or even the cause, of the 'underachievement' of boys. We are also aware that there are continuing, specific gender differences in schooling some of which amount to inequality and that their frontier is merely a moving one for women in higher education and the labour market and girls' access to 'hard' science, technology, engineering and the like. We are also aware that the nature of ethnic diversity and its educational concomitants are complex with respect of families, language, communities, religious, cultural and school experiences. The 'over achievement' of some groups is as marked as the 'underachievement' of others, for whom the mirror appears to be cracked. All that we would say is that the experience of gender and ethnicity is necessarily always mediated by class, as the literature clearly shows. Much of the post-structuralist work, particularly on the inscription of gender subjectivity and identity, has been extremely valuable but it might tell us more about their formation if it had a more adequate language for articulating generating principles and the encoding of identity within and through the organisational, curricular and pedagogical structures of schooling.

Our focus is almost exclusively on secondary schools and, once again, our rationale is space and the availability of literature on class reproduction. Pre-nursery and primary schooling experience matter greatly in respect of social and educational reproduction. The key text throughout the inter-war period of the all-age (5–14) elementary school system, even after the Board of Education had abandoned issuing its Codes in 1926, was its *Handbook of Suggestion for Teachers*, whose last edition was issued by HMSO in 1937 and reprinted in 1944. Its spirit was kept alive in textbooks for trainee teachers for many years after. While central government had given up its right to determine the elementary curriculum, in John White's view (1975), probably out of a combination of fear of a future Labour government radicalising the curriculum and so as to make more difficult the prospect of universal secondary education, the 1937 Prefatory Note to the *Handbook* reminded its readers 'that each teacher shall think for himself' (p. 3). Its subject directions were remarkably explicit for the teaching of 'ordinary', 'dull' and 'backward' children, from nursery to senior school stages, from health and physical training to mathematics. The *Handbook* devoted 30 pages to gardening, 61 pages to practical arts and crafts, 130 pages to all practical or manual activities and three pages to science. Its only reference to 'class' was as 'the most familiar of all school groups' (p. 30). Children are gender free but referred to as male until girls develop 'special needs' in the Senior School.

The Plowden Report (Central Advisory Council for Education (CACE), 1967), the touchstone of official 'progressivism', studiously avoided class as a category, although its second volume contained major appendices reporting specifically commissioned survey work packed with it. Len Marsh, one of the great modernisers of 1960s primary teacher education, produced *Alongside the Child in the Primary School* (1970) and *Being a Teacher* (1973) without affording class a single mention. In primary and secondary classroom studies, class was largely the discovery of qualitative researchers from the early 1970s onwards. Higher education has been until very recently a largely unresearched area from the point of view of sociological perspectives on policy; though its growth and change from the 1960s has been remarkable. At each advance in expansion and scope, from a system taking 5 to 40 per cent of the cohort, middle-class students' share of places as always stayed ahead and is highly dominant in our elite institutions while lower working class prospects have actually declined in both respects. A consideration of Further Education is also absent, although, as the current site of the victory of generic modes of pedagogic discourse, it is of the greatest interest.

Finally, our greatest regret is that we stay out of classrooms, which is where the work of reproduction mainly occurs in education and to which policy has now directly penetrated, albeit mainly at the primary level. If things are to change in terms of class chances, it is here that they will do so, through the elaboration of pedagogic forms which, once more in Bernstein's terms, enable reflection 'on what is to be acquired and how it is to be acquired' (Bernstein, 1996: 8). But students can only learn how to learn and to distinguish between their local and wider worlds when knowledge, resource and access conditions provide a context which is appropriate to them in all sorts of conditions. Our hope is that the rather narrow focus that we take will show how resilient patterns of privilege are and shed some light on what is prerequisite to lessening old injury and preventing new excess. We attempt to make some small amend for our omissions by offering a final chapter that takes the form of suggestions for further reading.

2 Framing equality?
The Education Act, 1944

Introduction

Analysts refer to policy frameworks as linking ideologies, political preferences groups and institutions to programmes of reform, often claiming to aim at greater equality. We have chosen to begin our account by examining those which lay behind the Education Act, 1944 for two main reasons. First, in selecting a piece of legislation that clearly 'made a difference' to the provision of British schooling we hope to emphasise both the historical and geographic dimensions of policy frameworks which are constituted in specific historical conditions and in particular sites. Second, the 1944 Act also illustrates their continuity, for not has it only provided the structure within which the very great majority of families, students and teachers have experienced schooling in Britain over the last six or so decades, but it still exerts a powerful influence on the institutional features of the contemporary British educational landscape.

The majority of us have passed through at least two phases of education, primary and secondary, designed, in Durkheim's (1961) terms, to make us more similar before making us more different. Primary schools have come to offer environments predicated upon children as developmental beings where they acquire key attributes of literacy, numeracy and the knowledge that the world can be a tricky, complex and sometimes confusing and upsetting place. Some people, including the authors, went on to benefit from selective secondary education, while most of our parents and some of our siblings and school friends did not. Some of us went to mixed schools, while others attended single sex schools. Others variously experienced the enormous benefit or conditional blessing of comprehensive secondary education while the prospects for many of getting on in the world were greatly constrained by being placed in schools where opportunities to achieve qualifications required for further and higher education were limited or simply unavailable. Any discussion of recent or contemporary policy in pursuit of equality, then simply has to begin with a consideration of the 1944 Act, whose consequences also provided a foundational object of study in the intellectual field of British sociology of education.

We have arranged the remainder of this chapter into three parts. The first part briefly discusses the idea of policy frameworks in relation to a Bernsteinian approach. The second part outlines key features of the 1944 Act and examines the distribution of power and control in British education after 1944. The third part introduces the tripartite system of secondary education that emerged following the 1944 Act as LEAs sought to carry out their duties under it and begins a preliminary discussion about its social consequences.

Policy frameworks

Policy by definition arises out of ideas and struggles of the past and seeks to shape social developments in the future. In the real world policies originate, operate and are made effective by ensembles of institutions or agencies and the actors working within them. They may be pushed for by departments of state, trade unions, churches, or other agencies within civil society, such as employers' federations or environmental or anti-capitalist protest groups. They can be thought of as outcomes of contested preferences expressed within the state and civil society, some of which go forward as practical programmes involving the allocation or reallocation of resources. Their strength or significance tends to lie in the extent to which resources are redefined or redirected to meet them, whether in health, education, policing, wherever. Each of these statements raises research-able questions about the origin of polices and why they take the forms that they do. Who are the players in a policy arena? Which resources are distributed, on what scale and to whom? Who are the beneficiaries and non-beneficiaries?

What is also the case, however, is that polices, in the form of practical pro-grammes emanating from government departments, take on particular characters and directions that often prove to be remarkably durable and difficult to change. Much of this has to do with the specific institutions through which policies operate and which imbue them with their particular values, purposes, processes of implementation and judgements about their relative effectiveness. We must also recognise that we live in a world where what 'is' slips easily into what 'ought to be', not only for those who win but also those who may lose as a result of particular arrangements (Skocpol, 1992).

Other contemporary social theorists, such as Steinmo *et al.* (1992) made much the same judgement when they argued that 'institutions matter'. Let us explain this idea a bit further because it is central to our account. Institutions are constituted by rules, regulations and procedures and these, in turn, regulate who can participate in their programmes and activities. Hospitals, for example, are defined by the existence of medically qualified staff making judgements about patient care. For instance, not just anyone can conduct operations, declare someone dead or suture wounds. Schools are, in the main, staffed by qualified teachers who play out rules about which students are to receive what contents, forms of instruction and evaluations, when, by what means and where. While these rules partly involve judgements of their own making they are also more or less determined by others, following rules made earlier and elsewhere. In Bernstein's terms, they work within particular pedagogic discourses determined by the outcomes of struggles for control of the pedagogic device.

Liberal democracy itself is predicated upon a right to vote but voting rights are carefully delineated. The age of majority may confer the right to vote, but it is exercised only within a designated geographical area, a constituency and only for registered parties at fixed intervals during declared election periods. The rules are different in each liberal democracy and these, in turn, give each of them their separate identity. Such rules define not only who can participate in elections, but also more generally the relationship between the governed and their governors. The rules of education systems also differ and their characters vary while, within each one, 'tradition' is often at a premium within individual and across different types of schools. It is precisely for these sorts of reasons that it is argued that 'institutions matter'.

As we use the term, then, policy frameworks are fundamentally ensembles of institutions that interpret and translate popular, bureaucratic and political preferences, ideas and ideologies into practical programmes that regulate the distribution of economic, social and cultural resources. 'Regulation' is never innocent, involving both the power that generates it and the control that it exercises. We emphasise the social functions of institutions whose rules and regulations have real social consequences. The ensembles of institutions that constitute policy frameworks are matters for empirical determination, as are how changes occur and in what direction. In investigation and analysis to determine which are involved, how and which are pre-eminent, we are aware that ensembles are historically and geographically defined.

In Bernstein's (1990, 1996) terms, we distinguished in Chapter 1 between the origins, elaboration and delivery of policy contents. While no policy item has ever sprung full grown from the brow of even the cleverest or most determined ministers, governments (or the state) *produce* them, very often after complex processes of pressure, advice seeking and consultation. They are then normally subject to complex processes of fleshing out, being given substance, or *recontextualised* by specialised agencies created by or linked to the state or who thrive by doing its business. They are then *reproduced* by organisations and agents specially charged to do so. In terms of British educational institutions, if we think of the successive levels of the state centred on a Ministry responsible to Parliament, whose name has changed many times in recent years (currently it is called the Department for Education and Skills (DfES)) as our policy *producer*, then beneath it sits a complex group of *official recontextualising* agents. These are mainly quangos who specialise in curricular, assessment and inspectorial fields, as well as *pedagogic* agents, ranging from publishing houses and university Schools of Education to teacher associations all of whom shape and define policy content and expected practice. The *reproducers* of policy contents are local authorities, schools and teachers.

Research and experience shows that not only is there no neat insulation between these levels or categories, but there is inherent and chronic difficulty as to how clearly or completely one level 'reads' the meaning and intention of others. Even when policies are not unclear or contradictory, which they frequently are, their meanings and requirements change and elaborate over time as institutions work on understanding and delivering them. There is resistance and struggle, as well as compliance, likely at all levels of the process, from the Commons to the classroom.

The 1944 legislation

Looking back at contemporary debates in the 1940s, two great themes animated discussions about what education should look like in the postwar period. There was overwhelming concern to create a more unified national system, providing a basis for the education of all children within a broadly common state system. This was intended to address somewhat chaotic pre-war arrangements, made worse by wartime destruction, evacuation and shortage, where schooling was provided by all-age elementary schools where children moved between 'standards' or grades. There was a tiny minority exiting at the 11+ stage, having successfully 'passed the scholarship' for entry to fee-paying grammar schools and 'public' schools (elite, private day and boarding schools) and even fewer to local authority centre schools. In particular, there was a more specific and even more urgent agreement about the construction of a system of universal secondary education. This latter reform was intended to address popular sentiments and cross-party consensus that the existing system was both inequitable and wasteful of talent, as well as unsuited to the needs of a changing economy

The social justice arguments for the extension of secondary education had been set out by R. H. Tawney in a party political pamphlet entitled *Secondary Education for All: A Policy for Labour* published in 1922. Tawney advocated two phases of compulsory schooling, each with dedicated schools, primary and secondary, that should be made available, universally and free, replacing the existing system of:

> elementary education for nine tenths of children and secondary education for the exceptionally fortunate or the exceptionally able [and thus] we need to envisage education in two stages in a single course which will embrace the whole development of childhood and adolescence up to sixteen and obliterate the now vulgar irrelevance of class inequality and economic pressure in a new system.
>
> (Tawney, quoted in Silver, 1973: 8)

Tawney made his arguments in a world where secondary education was either privately provided or made available to the less well off via the 1907 Free Places Scheme. Under its arrangements schools could have fees remitted for poor but able students if those selected from local authority establishments composed at least 25 per cent of their intake. These 'scholarships' were not means tested so that students were admitted strictly on a meritocratic basis without regard to parental income or standing. A later 'direct grant' scheme introduced by a Labour government replaced Free Places with a means tested Specialist Places Scheme in 1932 (Blackburn and Marsh, 1991). Tawney's criticism of the existing system of secondary education noted that it was available only to those who could afford fees or with sufficient ability to earn scholarships to pay them. It was a system that favoured what he called 'well to do parents able to pay fees' enabling 'their children to go to public secondary schools on easier intellectual terms than the children of poor parents who can enter them only on free places' (Tawney, quoted in Silver 1973: 8). Paradoxically, however, the later Specialist Places arrangement made matters worse as means testing in practice excluded many working-class children whose families hitherto had not been required to pay (Blackburn and Marsh, 1991).

Tawney also drew unfavourable comparisons between Britain and the USA claiming that, in the latter, 28 per cent of students progressed from primary to secondary education compared with 10 per cent in the UK, the majority of whom left school soon after their fourteenth birthday, that is, after three years of secondary schooling. Moreover, while 10 per cent was the average figure for students transferring from British primary to secondary schools, in some areas it was as low as 0.2 per cent. In his view this was 'hardly distinguishable from no provision at all' (Tawney, in Silver, 1973: 17). This system, he concluded, was not only unjust but wasteful of talent and, therefore, inefficient and harmful to economic development. These broad themes were taken up by successive official reports on school reform published prior to 1944, all setting the groundwork for the reconstruction of education.

In its boldness of its vision, the Education Act, 1944 may be set alongside the creation of the National Health Service in 1946 and the expanded system of public welfare as one of the key elements of the post war welfare state. Its principal features are well-known so we shall not rehearse them in detail here. It established a system of free, compulsory education for 5–14-year-olds (a leaving age to be raised in due course to 16) divided into primary and secondary phases, with transfer taking place at age 11. In a less well-known provision the Act placed a duty on newly created LEAs to offer part-time education for all young people up the age of 18 years. Within the competing demands of rebuilding postwar Britain, priority was given to this compulsory phase of education so that the post-compulsory phase of the Act were not put into effect. More broadly, the legislation constituted the distribution of power and control within the education system that broadly remained intact almost into the new millennium.

A governing partnership?

Although the passage below is often cited, it is worthwhile recalling how power was distributed by the 1944 legislation. Section 1 of the Act provided for the appointment of a Minister:

> whose duty shall be to promote the education of the people of England and Wales and the progressive development of institutions devoted to that purpose and to secure the effective execution by local authorities under his

control and direction, of the national policy for providing a varied and comprehensive education service in every area.

(Education Act, 1944: S.1)

In effect, the Act created a Ministry, with a budget drawn from public taxation, charged with responsibility for providing a national system of education. It also established LEAs; geographical administratively entities, which had responsibilities placed upon them by the Act to plan and provide schools, teachers and associated services for all children of compulsory school age in their boundaries. LEAs were also required to appoint a chief education officer and, in effect, establish a bureaucracy to oversee local arrangements for schooling. The system that emerged was commonly described as 'a national system but locally administered'. To what extent, though, did the legislation create a devolved system of education? Did the Act effectively lead to a concentration of power at the centre or, as many, including numerous government education ministers believed, a system of decision making that provided ministers and their officials with few levers with which to regulate the direction of education? The latter was certainly a view shared by Labour education ministers, such as Fred Mulley, Shirley Williams and Gerry Fowler up to three decades later. Mulley once mused that the only direct powers he could exert over schools was to order the dismantling of old air raid shelters in school playgrounds (Maclure, 2000). Another interpretation of these arrangements advanced by Kogan (1971, 1975) argued that educational policy emerged as a settlement between three key agencies, the Department of Education, the Association of Local Education Authorities and the National Union of Teachers, the dominant teacher association. In both views, decision making rested upon the notion of 'partnership' within which the powers of ministers and their officials' powers were strongly circumscribed.

For the period 1944–76 there were historically specific requirements and circumstances that sustained the conditions for such partnership. Toby Weaver, a senior figure in Department for Education and Science (DES) before becoming a policy scholar, described the relationship in the following terms:

> The LEAs are clients, but also less and at the same time much more than clients. They are clients in that it is the responsibility the department [the Department for Education and Science] to minister to their needs through the provision of services and resources. They are somewhat less than clients in that [...] they are in a number of ways subject to direction and control the Secretary of State. They are much more than clients in that the primary responsibility for most of the public provision of education rests with them and they bear a considerable portion of the cost and have a substantial share in the formulation of execution of national policy. It is these three characteristics that led the DES itself and most [...] witnesses to describe the LEAs individually and collectively as its partners.
>
> (Weaver, 1986: 37)

LEAs raised some of the revenue required for education and enjoyed considerable scope for independent action while being accountable to the Education Secretary for the character and quality of education provision in their area. The accountability system was relatively weak, initially based on school development plans that the DES monitored and, where appropriate, would require LEAs to adjust or amend. Although Weaver spoke of LEAs as 'clients' there was considerable latitude for them to develop arrangements in response to already existing patterns of educational provision, the preferences of elected members, administrators and local communities. It was a structure that permitted local variation to develop within an overall, national framework. For example, with respect of the age of school transfer and the timing and character of secondary reorganisation. LEAs were obligated to find school places efficiently for children of compulsory school age. Most chose to work with the grain of what was already available in their administrative areas, in effect reflecting patterns of pre-war arrangements. The mixture of patterns that developed of LEA/church, selective/non-selective, selective/all-ability and mixed or single sex schools varied from LEA to LEA. Chances of going to an academically selective grammar school were far greater in some areas than others and generally there were more places for boys than girls who had to secure higher test results than boys at 11+ in order to secure places, although precise figures of their performance differences are difficult to obtain. We may take this imbalance as one of the consequences of pre-1944 beliefs that academic education was wasted on girls whose destiny lay in marriage, the home and the domestic economy.

There was one other group of important participants, though not explicitly referred to as 'partners' in the postwar reconstruction and the form that it took. These were the churches. Prior to 1944 about one-third of all schools were church affiliated, an integral part of local systems of education and, in some rural areas, the only kind of school within easy reach of many families. Considerable time and energy was absorbed in the creation of the 1944 Act seeking some kind of settlement with the Church of England, whose schools were most numerous and the Catholic Church about their continuing participation in local, compulsory education (Gosden, 1976). The compromise agreed enabled church schools to elect to become fee-paying or assume 'voluntary status', receiving state funding and becoming, in effect, what was part of the state or maintained sector while retaining autonomy over matters of admission and governance.

This was quite unlike arrangements, say, in France or the USA where there is a strict separation between church and state and where it is forbidden to fund church schools from state taxation revenues. Churches could elect for their schools to become 'aided', which required them to raise 50 per cent of all capital cost of new buildings, refurbishment or repairs and have fewer LEA nominees on their governing bodies. Or they could opt for 'controlled' status, with increased LEA participation in their governance and all capital and recurrent costs, such as teacher salaries met from public funds. Nearly all Roman Catholic and about one-third of Anglican schools adopted the more expensive and autonomous 'aided' status, the rest forming the core of voluntary controlled schools. Church schools have continued to increase in number from 1944 until the present (Maclure, 2000: x) and current policy encourages their further growth. However, it remains a curious feature of educational analysis in the UK that little attention has been paid to participation of faith-based institutions in the policy-making arena.

During this period of partnership, extraordinary autonomy was enjoyed by both schools and educators in the determination of curriculum content and pedagogy. This was relatively new-found in primary schools, where the prescriptive influence of the *Handbook for Teachers* published by the Board of Education for elementary schools lingered on long after its final re-issue in 1944 and where preparing children for the 11+ dominated until local reorganisations had been achieved in most authorities. In secondary schools central specification of the curriculum had remained until 1944 but subject departments had now come to exert a major responsibility for the content, sequence and pacing of curriculum material and a large measure of control over pedagogic strategies and pupil grouping arrangements. This diminished in examination classes where syllabuses were effectively driven by examination boards controlled in the main by particular, or groups of, universities. Teachers were separately represented on national bodies, such as the Schools' Council, whose task it was to advise on examinations and to fund national curriculum projects, mainly oriented toward the perceived needs of a changing secondary system. The presence of Her Majesty's Inspectorate (HMI) effected linkage with the Department of Education. The DES and, indeed, the majority of LEAs' view was that curriculum and pedagogy were matters primarily for professionals to determine and develop. For the best part of 40 years there were, then, what were regarded as perfectly 'natural', pragmatic reasons why LEAs, teachers and central government accepted these arrangements that gave unique degrees of freedom to the pedagogic recontextualisers while the ORF stayed out of determining curriculum and pedagogy.

Maclure (2000) suggests that, for central policy administrators, the huge and complex task of providing 7.5 million pupil places plus recruiting and sustaining an estimated 70,000 teachers to cope with the increased number of students in, or about to enter, the system in the 1940s and 1950s were overwhelming pre-occupations. These figures included increases arising from the 'baby-boom' and the requirement to stay on at school beyond the age of 14 years. The school leaving age was finally raised to 16 in 1973. These tasks involved programmes, such as an emergency teachers training scheme and resourcing the new primary and secondary schools. By the time a kind of equilibrium was struck, from ministers' point of view in the early 1970s, in the balance between school places, qualified teachers and student numbers, public debate began to turn its attention to curriculum issues and also to the powers that the state had at its disposal to intervene in the operations of schools. As it did so the apparent vulnerability of the notion of 'partnership' in the policy-making arena also became more evident.

One of the key factors in this change was the work of HMI, a professionally independent government agency whose primary task was to monitor the quality of educational provision and to provide central government with intelligence about the health of the system. HMI's main work had long consisted of highly intermittent 'general inspection' of schools. Its prestige and leadership had largely passed to new cadres of LEA advisors and inspectors whose contact with and 'feel' for schools were much closer and surer than their own. In the early 1970s, having allowed itself to drift toward oblivion, HMI, in league with elements in the DES, began a concerted drive to reinstate itself as their chief purveyor of guidance and advice, repositioning LEA inspectorates firmly as overseers of implementation. By the mid-1970s, attention had been drawn to shortcomings in the effectiveness and performance of the British education system in comparison with other national systems. Following publication of the first of the *Black Papers* (Cox and Dyson, 1969), the media frenzy accompanying the Bullock Report (Committee of Enquiry into Reading and the Use of English, 1975) inverting its claim that there had been no fall in standards of literacy and the circulation within the DES of the confidential *Yellow Book* in 1976 asserting 'industry's' needs for improved levels of maths and English (Benn and Chitty, 1996). Labour Prime Minister James Callahan indicted both teachers and schools as failing British industry, a charge which the ensuing Great Debate did nothing to dispel. On this basis HMI obtained resources to conduct two national surveys, Doomsday-like accounts of the pattern and quality of compulsory school provision. Its two reports, *Primary Education: A Survey by HMI* (1978) and *Aspects of Secondary Education in England: A Survey by HMI* (1979) provided evidence not only in variation of pupils experience of education but also of the wide and sometimes unacceptable variation in the quality of curriculum content and classroom practice. Diversity and unevenness in the system had also arisen because LEAs had adopted different strategies for the provision of secondary schools and these crucially regulated the structure of opportunities available to families. The days of partnership were numbered.

Tripartism: a very British settlement?

We have spent some time discussing the governance and administration of education after 1944 because, as we noted earlier, they relate directly to a way in which the second broad purpose of the Act, 'secondary schools for all', was realised. While the 1944 Act required that all children should move into secondary education at age 11, precisely what form would be available to them had been a source of debate since Tawney's pamphlet in 1922. By 1944, two principles had been established in a series of official reports. First, secondary education was to be based on meritocratic principles. Talent or ability, would be the determinants of pupil access, progress and success and not ability to pay. For this reason, secondary education was to be free, so that fees and special places examinations which had enabled selective student take-up of free places were abolished. Second, official thinking about the form of provision had settled on the principle that 'the child is at the centre of education' and, so far as humanly possible, all children should receive the type of education for which they were suited (*Education Reconstruction*, 1943, Paragraph 27, cited in Halsey *et al.*, 1980: 27). These outwardly child centred sentiments, however, became embedded in Circular 73, 1945 issued in December by central government and giving guidance to LEAs, the effect of which was to propose that providing three different kinds of schools for children of dissimilar kinds of aptitudes and talents would requite their obligation under the Act (Benn and Chitty, 1996). That central government and its advisers adopted this so-called 'tripartite system' in effect meant defeat for those who had argued in the pre-war years for a system based on 'the common school' or, in the language of the time, 'multilateral' schools.

The 1944 Act itself did not specify the introduction of tripartite arrangements. It actually required local education authorities to provide a system which would enable students to engage in:

> a variety of instruction and training as may be desirable in view of their ages their abilities and aptitudes and of the different periods which they may be expected to remain at school, including practical instruction and training appropriate to their respective needs.
>
> (Halsey *et al.*, 1980, p. 29)

However, the apparent neutrality of the legislation masked other compelling evidence that a tripartite education system remained official policy for the next twenty years. For example, Gareth Elwyn Jones's (1990) account of central government's response to the school development plans that LEAs were required to submit in the wake of the Act provided a detailed account of the extent to which Whitehall delayed and frustrated those plans which did not put selection at their centre. What, however, were the origins of the idea of different schools for children of different kinds of ability?

Practical and policy preferences for a tripartite system emerged at the confluence of four lines of contemporary circumstances and thought. First, they were driven by sheer administrative pragmatism, of working with the grain of what existed on the ground. Grammar schools existed within most boundaries of the new LEAs and were often the most prevalent form of secondary education so this was a convenient place to commence the design of new systems. Second, there were politicians and civil servants, such as the authors of *Education Reconstruction*, whose foremost apparent concern was to preserve the grammar schools because they believed they had the important social function of preparing tomorrow's leaders. These schools represented 'the gold standard'. Secondary education for all, meritocracy, and modernisation were principles broadly accepted by what we might refer to as the political class but those objectives had to be achieved within a framework of preserving the grammar schools and, thus, preserving also the principle of selective education. Third, there was the idea of modernisation. Whatever direction secondary education took, from the 1920s onward, there was a view that it had to address the needs of the changing economy.

The skills base of a modern industrial structure had to be created via secondary schools. This strand of thought is probably best represented in the Spens Report (Ministry of Education, Consultative Committee on Secondary Education, 1939), which argued for the establishment of technical education and technical schools in the new phase of education. Fourth and most ideologically characteristic, underpinning the proposed new arrangements was the belief that there were different kinds of natural talents that could be identified with some precision and these could be matched to particular kinds of curriculum and pedagogy. The combination of the strands of thinking appear in an official report published by the Committee of the Secondary School Examinations Council (1943), also known as the Norwood Report whose authors also proposed three different kinds of schools, grammar, technical and 'modern secondaries'. The process of allocating students to the right school would be conducted by their classification based:

> not on the results of a competitive test, but an assessment of the individual aptitudes largely by such means as school records, supplemented, if necessary, by intelligence tests, due regard are being had to their parents' wishes and careers that have in mind.
>
> (Norwood, quoted in Halsey *et al.*, 1980: 27)

The Report was most notable for its forthright statement of the assumptions upon which this tripartism was constructed:

> The evolution of education has in fact thrown up certain groups, each of which must be treated in a way appropriate to itself. Whether such groupings are distinct on strictly psychological grounds, whether they represent types of mind, whether the differences are differences in kind or in degree, these are questions it is not necessary to pursue. Our point is that rough groupings, whatever may be their ground, have in fact established themselves in general education experience, and the recognition of such groupings in educational practice has been justified both during the period of education and in the after-careers of these pupils.
>
> (Norwood, quoted in Silver, 1973: 79)

The identities and qualities imputed to the three categories of pupil and kinds of school described below were later settled upon in *Education Reconstruction* as official advice to the system and later embodied by the majority of LEAs in their grammar, secondary modern and, less frequently, technical schools. It could be taken that:

> English education has, in practice, recognized that the pupil who is interested in learning for its own sake, who can grasp an argument or follow a piece of connected reasoning, who is interested in causes, whether on the level of human volition or in the material world, who cares to know how things came

to be as well as how they are, is sensitive to language as expression of thought, to a proof as a precise demonstration, to a series of experiments justifying a principle: he is interested in relating unrelated things, in development, in structure, in a coherent body of knowledge. He can take a long view and hold his mind in suspense; this may be revealed in his work or in his attitude to his career. He will have some capacity to enjoy, from an aesthetic point of view, the aptness of a phrase or the neatness of the proof. He may or may not be good with his hands or may not; he may not may not be a good mixer or a leader or a prominent figure in activities athletic or other.

Such pupils, educated by the curriculum commonly associated with the grammar school, have entered learned professions or have taken up higher administrative or business posts. Whether the curriculum was designed to produce men of this kind we need not inquire; but the assumption is now made, with confidence that for such callings a certain make up of aptitudes and capacities is necessary and for such make up may for educational purposes constitute a particular type of mind.

Again, the history of technical education has demonstrated the importance of recognising the needs of the pupil whose interests and abilities lie markedly in the field of applied science or applied art. The boy in this group has a strong interest in the direction and often necessary qualities of mind to carry his interest through to make it his life work at whatever level of achievement. He often has an uncannily insight into the intricacies of mechanism whereas the subtleties of language construction are too delicate for him. To justify itself to his mind, knowledge must be capable of immediate application, and the knowledge and its application which most appeal to him are concerned with the control of material things. He may have unusual or moderate intelligence: where intelligence is not great, a feeling of purpose and relevance may enable him to make the most of it. He may or may not be good at games or other activities.

[…]

Again, there has in later years been recognition, expressed in the framing of curricula and otherwise, of still another grouping of pupils and another grouping of occupations. The pupil in this group deals more easily with concrete things than with ideas. He may have much ability, but it will be the realm of facts. His interest is in things as they are; he finds little attraction in the past or with the slow disentanglement of causes or movements. His mind must turn its knowledge or its curiosity to immediate test; and his test is essentially practical. He may see along one line study of interest and outstrip his generally abler fellows in that line; but he often fails to relate his knowledge or skill to other branches of activity. Because it is interested only in the moment he may be incapable of a long series of connected steps; relevance to present concerns is the only way of awakening interest, abstractions mean little to him. Thus it follows that he must have immediate returns for his effort, and for the same reason his career is often in his mind. His horizon is near and within a limited area his movement is generally slow, though it may be surprisingly rapid in seizing a particular point and in taking up a special line. Again he may or may not be good with his hands or sensitive to music or art.

Within this group of pupils mental make-up does not show at an early stage pronounced leanings in a way comparable with that of the other groups which we indicated. It is by no means improbable that, as the kind of education suitable for them becomes more clearly marked out and the leaving age is raised, the course of education may become more and more supple and flexible with a result that particular interests and aptitudes may be enabled to declare themselves and the given opportunities for growth. That a development of this kind yet lies to a great extent in the future does not preclude us from recognising the existence of a group whose needs require to be met in as definite a manner as those of other groups.

(Norwood, quoted in Silver, 1973: 79–81)

These phrases also appear in an official postwar Ministry pamphlet, *The New Secondary Education* (Ministry of Education, 1947) whose purpose was to describe and justify tripartite secondary schools. The categories, however thin their evidential basis was for their existence or, indeed, what may now appear to be their absurdity, had real consequences, providing the intellectual and educational basis of allocating children with purported different capabilities to separate and different forms of secondary education. It will also be apparent that identities were constructed around boys and a presumed division of labour that was profoundly male.

Within the guidelines of this non-legislative framework which advised LEAs that their obligations under the Act could be requited by their adoption, the tripartite system rolled out in a piecemeal fashion. Each LEA adopted and adapted it to their local circumstances. The chances of obtaining a grammar school education varied considerably from LEA to LEA. As Floud and Halsey (1961: 7) noted 'it is a notorious feature of British education that grammar school provision varies from over 50 per cent in a Welsh county to 10 per cent in a Northern industrial town'. They also reported that small fluctuations in the birth rate regulated the proportion of children able to take advantage of secondary education. They noted, for example that, in 1952, boys in south west Hertfordshire had to achieve IQ test scores of 114 to enter grammar school, but that by 1953 pupils achieving this score were not offered places and that by 1954 they were only offered to students with a score of 116 or above (Floud and Halsey, 1961: p 214). The rise in the required score was a direct outcome of the growing scarcity of places. For purposes of allocating children to secondary school, LEAs fell back upon varied combinations of attainment and IQ testing as an administratively convenient way of addressing the tension between limited availability of grammar and technical school places and parents seeking them for their children.

Tests, taken in the last year of primary school at age 11 for grammar and usually later for a transfer to technical schools, more or less sealed the educational and occupational chances of cohorts of children until the broad availability of more or less all-ability comprehensive schools in the 1960s. In the two decades after the Act, 'the competitive tests' so deplored by Norwood, returned and intentions that fuller evaluations of pupil aptitude based on school reports seem to have been given little public importance. Moreover, in many LEAs primary school head teachers bore a heavy and remarkably unpublicised burden of allocating the selective places assigned to each of their schools to the particular children whom they thought most likely to benefit from grammar school education.

Given the local variation that we have noted above, which pupils went where? Central government had in mind that about 15 per cent of 11-year-olds should enter grammar school, another 15 per cent should be offered education in technical schools and the remaining 70 per cent should be educated in the new secondary moderns (Jones, 1990). Very few LEAs achieved even a 10 per cent intake to technical provision and many developed none at all. National provision never exceeded 4 per cent (Sanderson, 1994). The Crowther Report (Central Advisory Council for Education, 1959) reported that the percentage distribution of 11–18-year-olds in England and Wales by school type in 1958 was 60 per cent allocated to secondary moderns, 27 per cent to grammar, 5 per cent to all-age elementaries still to be phased out and 4 per cent each to technical schools and comprehensive/bilaterals. These figures have to be interpreted carefully as *participation* and not *intake* statistics. Unsurprisingly, as 71 per cent of all 15–18-year-olds were to be found in grammar schools their 27 per cent share of all 11–18-year-olds is greater than the 20 per cent of children gaining access to them at 11+. And as only about 15 per cent of secondary modern pupils stayed on to the age of 15 or beyond, the 70 per cent of pupils entering them at 11+ represented only 60 per cent of the whole age range in 1958. It is also worth noting that rather more pupils still remained in unreformed elementaries than were placed in either technical or the nascent comprehensive schools.

Officially, all schools and secondary students were to enjoy 'parity of esteem' within the system (Ministry of Education, 1947), but circumstances revealed otherwise. Spending per pupil was higher in grammar schools than in secondary modern schools for children of all ages, while a much higher proportion of their teachers had university degrees (Taylor, 1963). Grammar school pupils stayed on in school longer and more of them achieved credentials that enabled them to go into higher education. It was calculated that in 1955, for example, about 28 per cent of grammar school students left school and entered full-time higher education, while 4 per cent of students from technical schools and 0.3 per cent of secondary modern schools did so. Secondary modern students were destined for the lower skilled and payment ranks of the labour market. For contemporary commentators, such as Olive Banks (Banks, 1955) it was the extent to which selective secondary education prepared and projected students into a hierarchical division of labour that made it so pernicious. Selection at age 11 destined some children for an education that was better resourced, more highly esteemed and carried its advantages into the labour market. For the majority the structure of opportunity presented limited horizons which had to be struggled with and managed as best as they could.

Conclusion

The 1944 policy framework was composed of two historically specific elements. The first was legislative in character and was concerned primarily with the formation of a national system of education within which there was a distribution of power and control between central government, LEAs and schools, including the churches as major players. We suggested that this gave rise to considerable local variation in the kinds of schools that parents were able to choose between. It was a system that granted schools and teaches substantial professional autonomy over who got what in terms of the sequence, pacing and assessment of school knowledge. The second element of the framework was composed of non-legislative guidelines embedded in official reports that gave rise to the near-universal establishment of bi- or tripartite secondary education. Official discourse gave an inescapable administrative steer to LEAs to adopt selective forms of secondary education. This was consolidated by a Ministry empowered to shape local arrangements via its administration of LEA development plans and able to frustrate local attempts to introduce multilateral or all-ability schools. The non-legislative side of the framework proved to be a powerful way of regulating the system and its success in doing this is evident in the extent to which LEAs adopted or were strongly steered into arrangements for selective secondary education. Class dominance of the system was 'easy' and 'natural' so that for many it appeared neutral. The new arrangements were to provide only a 'ladder of opportunity' capable of being ascended by students from what sociologists in the 1960s were to refer to as educative families. These would include the brightest and best from the working classes.

3 Selection, class and opportunity

Introduction

Between 1945–7 the principle of secondary education for all was realised within the framework proposed by official pre-war reports. In terms of these reports, who should go where sometimes seemed rather more important than the principal purpose of providing universal, free secondary schooling. They made specific recommendations that about 15 to 20 per cent of the secondary school population would benefit from academically selective education. The great majority of secondary school students were expected to attend either secondary modern schools or technical schools. All age elementary schools were progressively dismantled and replaced by local systems based of primary schools, whose pupils were usually selected either to enter grammar schools, secondary modern schools or, usually later, technical schools. In some areas, particularly where the local stock of school buildings made the provision of larger establishments infeasible, middle schools bridged the gap between primary and secondary stages. In some LEAs, such as Alec Clegg's West Riding, they were also intended to mitigate the consequences of early selection. In different authorities, age of entry varied between ages 8–10 and transfer to 'high school' between ages 12–14. Some patterns prolonged primary school practice and regulations, others embodied a secondary ethos. In 1985 those deemed primary schools formed less than 2 per cent of all primary schools in the UK, while the 2 per cent of students attending those deemed secondary schools grew to 7 per cent by 1986 (Statham *et al.*, 1989). In this chapter we focus on secondary school admissions and explore how the principle of 'secondary school for all' developed within a framework of academic selection, focusing particularly on the effects of the 11+, early leaving and staying on.

Selection and social class

Pre-war research provided some insights into likely patterns and to the groups which were likely to benefit most from the framework, establishing that grammar school and 'scholarship' places were held disproportionately by children from professional, middle-and lower middle-class families. Lindsay's 1926 study of the social composition of secondary schools in Warrington, Bradford, Oxfordshire and London, areas with a variety of occupational structures, concluded that children of unskilled and lowly paid workers, e.g. farm and casual labourers, had not benefited greatly from the scholarship system (Lindsay, quoted in Silver, 1973: 39). He found, for example, that only 40 schools out of 212 in his study sent scholarship or 'free placers' on to secondary schools and that the majority of these were located in well-to-do districts. In Liverpool, he reported that 'out of the 321 schools from which 'scholarship' or free places might have originated, 78 failed to nominate a scholar, 208 failed to win a scholarship and 115 did not win a free place' (op. cit.: 29).

In a later and equally ambitious study, Gray and Moshinsky (1938) attempted to calculate the proportions of fee and free place (from economically disadvantaged families) children of high ability, as measured by conventional IQ tests and by a device called the Index of Brightness and their relative likelihood of progressing to higher education. They concluded that, of students of similar ability, seven fee-paying students would go on to receive higher education for every one student receiving a free place. In other words, even where students were matched in terms of ability or capacity to benefit from selective education on the basis of the measures employed in the study, children from wealthier families were more likely to complete their schooling and move on to university. These earlier studies of academic selection began to document both the unequal class chances of entering secondary education and the differential advantages that home background conferred on students. They showed how social and economic inequality was both reflected in, and sustained by systems of secondary education that provided opportunities for a privileged minority. These early studies can be interpreted as some of the foundation stones of the sociology of education and reflect early and sustained interest in issues of selective schooling and its relationship to patterns of social inequality.

This was given new impetus after the introduction of the 1944 Act when politicians, policy makers and academics sought to explore the impact of the legislation on the structure of opportunities it afforded to the postwar generation of secondary school students. There was particular interest in the extent to which pre-war patterns had been interrupted or preserved. Academic selection in its postwar form came under three kinds of scrutiny. The first was a principled critique of a divided school system based on academic selection in preference to the idea of a 'common schools' which admitted students of all abilities and was closely tied to its community and within which students shared a similar experience of education. Simon's *Three Schools or One* (1948) was one such study. Her main concern, shared by teachers' associations and the Labour Party, was that a divided system not only reflected but was the cause of bitter class divisions. However, such a socialist critique of selection was not shared by the contemporary Labour government, or its Minister for Education, Ellen Wilkinson and deep ambiguity continued to mark official Labour attitudes to comprehensive schools It was such that Prime Minister Harold Wilson, even in the 1960s, promised that they would do no less than offer a good grammar school education for all.

While 11+ examinations relied almost everywhere on measures of attainment, mainly in English and Arithmetic, some LEAs additionally employed IQ testing. Psychologists, such as Vernon who were critical of IQ tests challenged their use as a means of distributing educational opportunities (Simon, 1953, 1971). In his synthesis of research on IQ tests, Simon noted that IQ was shown to vary, year-on-year, for individual children. Their capacity to predict who would and would not benefit from an academically selective education was somewhat limited. More tellingly, in light of the high stakes of 11+ examinations, coaching children in the techniques of test taking could also boost IQ. He cited Vernon's 1952 study where it was reported that about 17 per cent of an average class of children would be expected to achieve a score of 115, which was the threshold score for grammar school entry. After coaching, the average score could rise by as much as 15 points. This would be enough for half of the class to now qualify for grammar school places. Schools, which offered appropriate coaching and/or parents who were able to pay for it could, therefore, provide some children with advantages over others in the high stakes 11+ tests, whether attainment or IQ based.

There were also other problems with tests of general intelligence and their use in selecting categories of students with different aptitudes. One of the best studies of what such tests can and cannot do was Gould's (1981) *Mismeasure of Man*. In it he drew attention to the genesis of general tests. In practice, he argued, they were a misapplication of tests designed by Alfred Binet, the original aim of which was to identify a category of students with specific learning difficulties who would benefit from further support and extra resources. They were not, he argued, designed to classify with precision a range of different levels of ability in whole populations. The tests were also criticised for the cultural biases unwittingly built into them, especially but not exclusively, their linguistic elements. Neither linguistic nor figurative tests of general intelligence measured or identified some innate or unchanging quality of general intelligence but qualities tacitly acquired in home and community environments. Moreover, they recognised and rewarded features found in some environments and not others. This was what was meant by cultural bias.

The third and most telling critique of selection policy terms arose within the 'political arithmetic' style of analysis of educational policy. As its name suggests this approach employed numerical or quantitative data to analyse the effects of public, social and educational policies (Heath, 2000). The Gray and Moshinsky study exemplified this approach and interestingly was published in a collection of similar studies edited by Lancelot Hogben (1938) in a volume entitled *Political Arithmetic: A Symposium of Population Studies*. These studies had a policy 'bite' because they dealt in relatively simple numbers and proportions readily under-stood by those engaged in the wider arena of policymaking and policy analysis. These studies were also construed as sociological because they focused on social class inequalities in education, health, public services and welfare. For example, Gray and Moshinsky focused on grammar school access – who obtained places and who did not. To measure this they calculated from their sample schools the proportions or percentages of middle-class and working-class students, defined by paternal occupational status, placed in grammar, technical and non-selective schools. More sophisticated studies in this genre, of which we will give examples later, developed techniques which demonstrated the extent to which social class groups were over or under represented in grammar, technical and secondary modern schools. More recently policy analysts have employed 'odds ratios' (Heath, 2000) and 'segregation ratios' (Gorard, 2000; Gorard *et al.*, 2003). These are expressions of the likelihood of groups achieving access to services or to particular kinds of schools. They are all very similar in purpose to Gray and Moshinsky's techniques.

Selection, social class and school composition

The consuming issue for sociologists in Britain by the 1950s concerned the extent to which the 1944 legislation preserved the patterns observed in pre-war studies. Did the Act reduce or spread opportunities more widely, preserve pre-existing patterns of school composition or enable more working-class children to attend what became the elite section of state education, the grammar schools? Hilde Himmelweit's (1954) study of the impact of the 1944 Act and specifically tripartism was a contribution to David Glass's (1954) overarching research on social mobility in postwar Britain. Glass was a key figure both in studies of social mobility and in the political arithmetic approaches to public policy analysis. Himmelweit's research was based on questionnaires administered to 725 13–14-year-old boys, attending grammar and secondary modern schools in greater London. Schools were selected in London's predominantly working-class East End, a socially mixed area in South West London and in middle-class, suburban London. The boys were classified by their fathers' occupations and categorised into social class based on occupational prestige (see Table 3.1).

Himmelweit argued that for working-class boys to move upwards in status they must not only have the opportunity of attending grammar school but also pass the examinations that would successfully mark completion of their courses. She, therefore, hoped to compare the proportion of working-class children in

Table 3.1 Percentage distribution of sample by type of school and social status group

| Social status of pupils | Secondary | | | | | |
| | Grammar school | | Secondary modern | | Total | |
	%	No.	%	No.	%	No.
Middle class	21.7	72	5.9	23	13.1	95
Lower middle class	26.5	88	13.7	54	19.6	142
Upper working class	37.0	123	38.5	151	37.8	274
Lower working class	14.8	49	42.0	165	29.5	214
Total	100	332	100	393	100	725

Source: From Himmelweit, 1954: Table 1, in Silver, 1973: 123.

grammar schools and their examination performance with those of students from middle-class families. Her key findings were:

1   working-class children occupied nearly 52 per cent of grammar school places in her study. However, manual or lower working-class children, who constituted 29.5 per cent of her sample, were markedly under represented, gaining only 14.8 per cent of them, while occupying 42 per cent of secondary modern places;
2   upper working-class children were more adequately represented, forming 37.8 per cent of the sample and gaining 37 per cent of grammar school places. Middle-class children (13.1 per cent of the sample and gaining 21.7 per cent of places) were over-represented in grammar schools;
3   working-class children performed relatively poorly in attainment tests administered to determine who would obtain entry to grammar school. As they accounted for two-thirds of the total assessment package this was sufficient to exclude them from selective education;
4   168 boys out of the 725 in the sample with identical scores had been allocated to different schools, 69 to secondary modern and 89 to grammar. These over-achievers (the 89 boys placed in grammar schools) and under-achievers (the 69 boys placed in secondary modern schools differed by social class background. Only 12 per cent of over-achievers came from working-class backgrounds while 55 per cent were middle class. Only 12 per cent of under-achievers had middle-class backgrounds while 19 per cent came from non-manual and 39 per cent from manual backgrounds;
5   children from smaller families and eldest sons were more likely to be found in grammar schools;
6   none of the children in the sample had yet sat public exams (at that time this was the School Certificate) so that proper comparison across schools and between individuals was impossible. However, comparisons could be made of performance in those subjects that were in the curriculum of most grammar schools and so some impressionistic outcomes were reported. By and large, children from middle-class families were found more commonly at the top of the class lists of performance and less frequently among the bottom five; so that
7   overall performance at grammar school was associated more with social class than IQ test results at entry to school. In other words, family background, family culture, financial situation and teacher attitudes were regarded as the likely regulators of differentiated performance in school subjects.

   Based on the evidence of Himmelweit's study, the 1944 legislation had done little to reduce class advantages noted in pre-war studies. The under-representation of working-class students in grammar schools, many of whom were as able as some middle-class children, suggested that selection involved social and cultural processes, as well as educational assessments. Floud *et al.*'s (1956) now classic study of the social determinants of education selection provided further compelling evidence of the strong relationship between social class and differential access to selective and non-selective schools. They focused on secondary school provision in two contrasting regions, South West Hertford-shire (metropolitan, white-collar, suburban, middle class) and Middlesbrough (Northern, industrial, blue-collar, manual working class) between the years 1952–4. In the former, male entrants from families with professional and managerial backgrounds increased their grammar school entry share from 39.6 to 63.6 and those from supervisory and shopkeeping groups from 20.8 to 31.9 per cent. Over the same period the share of those from families in skilled and unskilled manual categories fell from 14.9 to 11.5 per cent. In other words, while boys from manual backgrounds took 42 per cent of the expanded number of grammar school places in South West Herts in 1950–3 (compared to16 per cent in 1934–8), a smaller percentage of them did so in Middlesbrough, where the pre- and postwar manual boys' shares of grammar school places were 46 and 44 per cent respectively while, for England and Wales in 1930–41 and 1946–51, Glass (1954) put them at 40 and 56 per cent (Floud, 1962). Floud *et al.*'s findings consolidated Himmelweit's results in showing close relationships between social class and opportunity to enter grammar school (Floud *et al.*, 1956; Himmelweit, 1954). Children from professional and other non-manual families (what was loosely referred to as 'middle class') dominated grammar school entry in this period. Equally telling was the decline in the proportion of working-class children entering expanded selective education that matched the sharp rise in students from middle-class backgrounds in the areas which they studied where they calculated that middle-class children were about ten times more likely to gain entry to grammar schools than those from unskilled manual families. 'Class chances' also varied from year to year. While the number of grammar school places tended to remain fixed year-on-year in any given area, variations in the number of eligible students at 11+ increased or reduced overall chances of entry. Moreover, the size of the 'pool of talent', the number of students with qualifying IQ or requisite 'ability', also changed, further increasing or reducing such opportunities.

Taking these features into account, Floud and Halsey (1961) concluded that working-class children found it progressively more difficult to gain grammar school places. Having begun their study by asking to what extent the 1944 Act had extended educational opportunities, being especially concerned about the effects on groups originally denied access to secondary education, they reported two broad findings. First, many more working-class boys than before had entered expanded secondary education and, as a result of fees being abolished, widening competition for more numerous grammar school places had led to many of them gaining entry. There was a closer relationship of ability to opportunity than ever before. Allowing for differences in their ability levels, working- and middle-class boys, as groups, got closer to their 'fair share' of grammar school places. But, at the same time, they concluded that in 1953 the proportion of boys of working-class manual backgrounds entering grammar schools at 12 per cent in Middlesbrough and 14 per cent in South West Hertfordshire remained at about the same proportion as in the period 1931–41. In the new competition for grammar school places working-class boys still lost out relative to the sons of middle-and lower middle-class families. Grammar schools traditionally had been at the service of the middle class and 1944 had not changed that. They remained predominantly middle-class institutions, which still 'assimilated' only a small minority of highly selected working-class students. Selective secondary education was failing to realise the potential of many. This 'social waste', they argued, 'is difficult to avoid so long as grammar school provision takes the relatively inflexible form of places in separately organised and housed schools, entrants to which are selected by competitive examination (Floud and Halsey, 1961: 214).

Olive Banks (1955: 242) shared their critique of grammar schools in her authoritative study of postwar secondary education, *Parity and Prestige*, in which she argued that the fundamental categorisation of three different kinds of children in the Hadow, Spens and Norwood Reports was psychologically and sociologically unsound and tripartism was a barrier to parity and prestige in a social structure where 'the prestige of the schools derives from the social and economic status of the occupations for which it prepares'. Both Floud *et al.* and Banks pointed the way forward to the desirability of multilateral or all ability secondary schools which would accommodate children across the ability range rather than their separation under variations of tripartitism in different institutions. But how did these authors see the relationship between tripartite education and the social and economic structure? Banks was unequivocal; grammar schools served to widen evident divisions of power and prestige in the social structure. For this reason she cautioned against the optimism of those who believed that multilateral schools would close gaps between social and occupational groupings in later life. At best, they could foster 'understanding between the different strata' (Banks, 1955: 245). The power of grammar schools lay in their capacity to confer on a few the credentials that provided access to positions of power and prestige in the occupational and social structure and not an education which was intrinsically better or more liberating. In the longer term, however, grammar schooling also presented policy makers with another difficulty. It came to define what was considered to be 'good education' through popular association with the characteristics of its highly visible, teacher led pedagogy, with strong subject boundaries and focus on obtaining high status credentials. It was unambiguously competence focused and attempts to modify its attachment to knowledge singulars and traditional forms of assessment were strongly resisted.

These early studies of academic selection and its effects placed themes, such as social justice, equity, equality of access and their consequences at the centre of the intellectual field of the sociology of education, though not at the heart of policy making. Their focus on how divisions in education both reflect and reproduce social and economic divisions remains one of the central concerns of the field though a topic that policy makers still tend to fall silent upon, preferring to talk of school effectiveness and improvement. The techniques employed in measuring who gained most benefit from the 1944 legislation and the piecemeal adoption of tripartism, in adjusted forms, are still employed today (Heath, 2000;

Blackburn and Marsh, 1991; Bynner and Joshi, 2002). In policy terms the studies provided the empirical basis on which parents, teachers associations, educational professionals and a variety of agencies in the PRF argued for change and for consideration to be given to multilateral or all-ability schools.

Greater equality of opportunity?

Did the Act achieve greater equality of opportunity, as those who were concerned to promote the cause of universal secondary education hoped it would? For some answers we turn to later studies which provide a longer view of its impact by Halsey, Heath and Ridge (1980) (hereafter, HHR) and Blackburn and Marsh (1991), a study which re-analyses the HHR data. Our account is, of necessity, brief so we cannot hope to map all the nuances of these important studies. In each, data is derived from the Oxford Mobility Study composed of a representative sample of just over 8,000 men in England and Wales, aged between 20 and 59, interviewed in 1972. The sample was divided into four 10-year birth cohorts, two of which entered school prior to the introduction of the 1944 Education Act and two afterwards. It was argued that this enabled measurement of any changes wrought by the Act on equality of opportunity (see Table 3.2).

Some explanation is required to interpret the table adequately. First, it employs a three class model, 'service' or professional managerial, 'intermediate' or smaller employer/self-employed/clerical and 'working' class which includes semi-skilled and non-skilled manual workers. Second, the notion of selective education has been broadened to include entry to grammar, technical and all fee-paying schools, including direct grammar schools and the elite boarding schools. What patterns emerge and what do they tell us about the impact of the Act?

First, the overall proportion of boys attending selective school had increased over the period, from 29.6 to 35 per cent. This was probably accounted for by an increase in the supply of places. Second, the chances of boys from service class families entering secondary education had remained remarkably stable, with in excess of two-thirds of them, across the period, attending such schools. Sons had broadly the same chances of admission to selective education as their fathers. These figures raise some interesting questions about the process by which the middle and professional classes continued to secure a privileged education. Third, and perhaps most depressing is that the chances of working-class boys entering

Table 3.2 Attendance at selective secondary schools (%)

| | Birth cohort | | | | |
Father's class	1913–22	1923–32	1933–42	1943–52	All
I, II (service)	69.5	76.7	79.3	66.4	71.9
III, IV, V (intermediate)	34.9	44.0	43.3	37.1	39.6
VI, VII, VIII (working)	20.2	26.1	27.1	21.6	23.7
All	29.6	37.0	38.8	34.8	35.0

Source: From Halsey, Heath and Ridge, 1980: Table 4.9, p. 63.

selective education actually fell in the period after the 1944 Act from 27.1 to 21.6 per cent. A larger proportion attended selective schools in the two birth cohort periods prior to the act. Moreover, using another measure, 'log distance' calculations, in the original study HHR also show that 'distance' or 'gap' between' service and working-class entry to selective education increased after three decades where the 'gap' had steadily closed, even when the overall number of students going into selective education had been taken into account. HHR noted that, 'These results are "surprising" and "depressing" from the point of view of the educational reformer' (HHR, 1980: 63) and they require a detailed explanation.

Much of their account is set out in terms of 'supply and demand', changes in population alongside availability of particular kinds of schools that drive the figures in Table 3.2. First, post-1944 population growth outstripped the supply of grammar and selective school places so that the overall proportions entering selective education fell. Second, far from expanding, technical schools fell in numbers and this had the effect of disproportionately reducing the numbers of intermediate and working-class children obtaining places in selective schools. Third, grammar schools offered free selective education to middle-class families who previously were ineligible for fee-waiver under the means tested 'special places' scholarship system or had entered private education. In the competition for relatively fewer and 'free' grammar school places, then, intermediate and working classes were squeezed out and was reflected in the increasing 'gap' between middle-class and working class successes in gaining selective school places after the introduction of the Act. There is later evidence from other studies (e.g. Edwards *et al.*, 1989) to support the broad thrust of this argument. The elite boarding schools became aware by the late 1960s that, in terms of relative performance, they were losing out to direct grant and local grammar schools and went into overdrive to reverse the perception that they were academies and finishing schools for ladies and gentlemen.

The more telling assessment that HHR make of the 1944 Act, however, raises a further general issue about educational reform policies. For them, it was an example of the fact that '(A)cts of parliament are as often legislative confirmation of socially accomplished fact as they are innovations in social practice' (HHR, 1980: 69). In their view, opportunities for social mobility via selective education had been made available prior to the 1944 Act to the point where working-class boys, at least, were successfully competing for grammar school places. Their conclusion on the overall effects of the 1944 Act was sobering as to:

> whether educational development and its legislative confirmation and completion in 1944 brought the country any nearer to meritocracy. Our verdict is that it did not. Making the contentious assumption that measured intelligence indicates meritocracy and it is an attribute of individuals independent of their class origins, it still turns out that meritocracy has been modified by class bias throughout the expansion of secondary opportunity.
> (HHR, 1980: 71)

This argument, couched primarily in terms of meritocracy, is one we can only agree with in light of other data we have presented in this chapter. However, in terms of 'innovation in social practice', aspect of legislation and educational policies, can the Act be regarded merely as confirming existing social facts? Two arguments call for a more optimistic evaluation. Whatever else the Act did, it entitled future cohorts of children to two phases of education, broadly aligned with cognitive developmental stages. This, in turn, encouraged innovation and experimentation within each phase both in terms of curriculum and pedagogy which, it can be plausibly argued, provided for a richer and varied education for a broader spectrum of children than previously. Second, as Blackburn and Marsh (1991) observed, the emphasis of the Act was on universal and not targeted provision. Within broadly social democratic societies, universal provision offers the general and democratic prospect of children, regardless of their social, economic and cultural background, experiencing education in common phases, if not in common schools and the prospect of social integration through some kind of common experience. They contended that universal provision was more likely to promote equality overall, 'other things being equal' (p. 530). In their recalculation of the data employed by HHR, they suggest that, had the 1944 Act not been introduced, the growing inequalities that the Oxford study reported would indeed have been very much worse. They argued that the Act

> reversed the general trend to inequality which was visible in the 1920s and 30s as those at the top increased their relative advantage over those immediately below them. In counterpoint, however, by replacing means-testing with universal provision, it increased inequality at the bottom, presumably by benefitting those who had previously been most sensitive to financial obstacles. The former effect outweighed the latter, so overall inequality declined; the decline was, however, not dramatic and must surely have been less than hoped for.
>
> The gains in equality did not last [...] the trend set by the Act was subsequently reversed. The number of selective places continued to grow throughout the 1950s and 1960s, but was outstripped by the 'baby boom' population [...] the effective value of social advantage became greater. The old inequalities reasserted themselves and indeed rose to higher levels than before.
>
> (HHR, 1980: 529)

It is probably fair to conclude that the framers of the 1944 Act could not and did not anticipate the postwar baby boom and the sharpened competition for places in the highly esteemed schools that resulted. Nor is it likely they anticipated the decline in the number of technical schools, nor did they have or attempt to collect reliable data on what parents actually wanted from the education system. The increasing desirability of selective education evidenced by middle-class pursuit of, and success in, its terms had one consequence that we have already noted: to promote the qualities of grammar school education as the equivalent of 'good' education, with consequences that bedevilled secondary education long after the demise of the tripartite system.

'Whatever Happened to the Likely Lads?'

To this point we have discussed the 1944 Act as it shaped school admissions. What happened to the first generations of children who were for the first time given the opportunity to stay and attend secondary schools? It is fair to say that the aspirations of those who supported universal secondary education were frustrated by the proportion of students who left school before completion of their secondary education. A decade after the Act, *Early Leaving* (1954) signalled official unease. This official report was based upon returns by headteachers on the 1946 intake in a stratified sample of 10 per cent of all grammar schools. This information was supplemented by material collected from youth club members and national servicemen conscripted into the armed forces. The term 'early leaving' seems to have been preferred in official and popular discourse to the more trenchant 'drop out' widely employed to discuss the same phenomena in American literature where it has been treated more urgently. The report addressed questions of who dropped out of secondary school and why. In summary it indicated, as Table 3.3 records, that working-class children were more likely to leave school before their middle-class counterparts and with fewer qualifications, even when they attended the same school. Girls were even more likely to drop out than boys, working-class girls faring slightly less well than their male peers with respect of early leaving and external examination results.

The authors of the report calculated that, of children who entered grammar school, more than half failed to obtain as few as 3 ordinary level passes (usually at age 16+) and, of these, more than half left before their fifth year. When children whose fathers were in unskilled occupational backgrounds were considered separately, the picture was even starker. About two-thirds of the this group left without achieving 3 ordinary level passes or better, and only about 1 in 20 went on to achieve two advanced or A-level passes. By any measure, this represented a phenomenal wastage rate amongst children chosen as capable of benefiting from an academically selective education. Early leaving or drop-out rates were also higher for girls and for boys. Extrapolating from the group's 1621 children, 921 of whom were from semi and unskilled backgrounds, *Early Leaving* concluded

Table 3.3 Proportions of 1946 recruits who left school at ages 15–18 (%)

Age	Professional and managerial	Clerical manual	Skilled manual	Semi-skilled	Unskilled	All
18+	34	10	4	2	1	8
17	17	9	3	2	1	5
16	24	22	15	11	6	15
15	25	59	78	85	92	72

Source: Central Advisory Council for Education (England), 1954, *Early Leaving*.

that 'it is illogical to admit 16,000 children to grammar schools and to accept without strenuous efforts to prevent it, that 9,000 will drop out or fail academically' (in Silver, 1973: 134). For working-class children, getting into grammar school was one achievement, staying there proved to be another.

What was striking about the *Early Leaving* Report, aside from the picture of wastage that it presented, was its attempt to engage in explanations of the patterns that were identified. It recognised that causal factors were likely to be complex and not fully understood. Nevertheless, it was to students' home backgrounds that its authors turned in search of an explanation, thereby foreshadowing a later corpus of work, produced by official inquiries and researchers, that sought explanations of differential middle-and working-class educational achievement, for example, the Crowther Report (CACE, 1959), Plowden Report (CACE, 1970), Douglas *et al.* (1968) and Jackson and Marsden (1966). The Plowden Report considered the physical environments in which children lived and worked, the proportion of families with working mothers and poverty levels. It also gave particular emphasis to what it called the 'outlook and assumptions' of parents and children from all walks of life, something that later became described as 'the culture' of the home and community. Floud *et al.* (1956, cited in Silver, 1973: 167) assumed their importance when they wrote:

> The precise nature of the hindrance placed by their home background in the way of educating working-class children in grammar schools urgently needs investigating both for its own sake as an immediate problem of education organization, and for the light it would throw on the problems in the possibilities of the comprehensive school. But in the long run, the problem must be viewed as part of the broader question of interaction of homes and schools generally – of the influence of the home at each social level on the educability of children in school of particular types and with particular traditions and aims.

The 'interaction' between home and school was set to become the key explanation for the relative performance of children from different social categories. The cultural logic of *Early Leaving* presumed that parents with grammar school backgrounds and higher levels of educational achievement created environments where staying on was an unquestioned social convention. This was not the case for families whose fathers were in semi-skilled and unskilled occupations, where such assumptions about staying on were less likely to exist and where parents were more likely to be neutral or to state that 'when to leave' was their children's decision. What emerges as an explanation is a 'deficit' account of working-class culture and environment; these families 'lacked' something that middle-class families had in abundance and it was this absence of the assumptive middle-class world of educational and social expectations that condemned their children to an early exit from the school and the lower rungs of the ladder of opportunity and upward social mobility. But much of this was supposition. The questionnaire surveys employed by the authors of the report did not address these issues directly.

Moreover, an alternative explanation in terms of the rationality of such behaviour, or the role of schools in engendering a differential response was virtually unthinkable.

Prominence was also given to parental attitudes when the Report, which was almost unique among contemporary discourse, turned its attention directly to the issue of girls. A greater proportion left school early and gained fewer qualifications than boys. Over 42 per cent from backgrounds where their parents were in unskilled occupations left before taking public examinations and only 6 per cent proceeded to A level, compared to 38 per cent and 7 per cent, respectively of boys. These girls were also seven times more likely to leave than their middle-class sisters and seven times less likely to make it into the sixth form. For the authors, a ready explanation could be given for such differential staying on rates. They argued that:

> It is common knowledge that many parents attach more importance to their sons' education than their daughters. The idea is not dead that a good education is wasted on a girl because she will get married and if the choice seems necessary between taking a girl or a boy from school it will usually be the girl who leaves. If the mother dies or falls ill or is overworked, a girl may be brought home to look after the family
>
> (*Early Leaving*, cited in Silver, 1973: 134)

Girls were doubly disadvantaged, with class and gender shaping their life chances, the former appearing to be the dominant influence. While the Report's authors emphasised the importance of the assumptive worlds of families in shaping opportunities and life chances, the labour market in postwar Britain continued to structure what families perceived to be possible and what was available to boys and girls.

While girls and their mothers made a brief appearance in *Early Leaving* and the 'sunken middle-class' mothers located by Jackson and Marsden leavened Northern working-class aspirations, they were mostly absent from the foundational texts of the sociology of education. In Banks (1955) they do not rate a mention in the index although a comparative study of girls' and boys leaving ages and their post-school destinations in the labour market is presented in the body of the text. That the narrow focus on fathers' occupations and boys' subsequent educational careers simplified sampling and data collection procedures is brought home with considerable clarity. We do not have nearly the same detailed, empirical data about how girls fared after the Act and such material is difficult to come by except in sources, such as Byrne (1978: 79), who recalled in this poignant memoir that:

> In 1945, a second shock changed my world and my outlook. Startlingly, I passed the scholarship. My father, still my legal guardian although he did not have custody of us, flatly refused to sign the necessary forms to allow my sister or I to take up our grammar school places – 'a waste of time

educating the girls' he said. In those days rules were rules. I owe to my mother's private education, her determination, her poise in adversity and her red tape cutting with two directors of education, my extended secondary education which has been a key to an exciting life. But just down the little country road ten-year old June, so much cleverer than I and mathematically very gifted, listened to her mother. 'I'm right sorry love, but your dad just won't let you go'. An inarticulate family with an unexpected chance they gave into conditioning which gave her brother Jem his city school place over his sister: she left at 15 to go into a factory.

In a narrative about class and gender this eloquently makes the point that there was a need for girls' own stories within studies that were relentlessly boy-focused.

Conclusion

The studies reported here and other contemporary and near contemporary investigations clearly demonstrated connections between the social structure and its education system. The manner in which the secondary school system was established demonstrated what we might refer to as the commitment of the political class to universalism, so long as the system identified, recruited and educated the most able, including their progeny, separately from the rest. With insufficiently rapid growth in the number of grammar school places, it was working-class children who lost out disproportionately in the competition for academically selective education. Broadly the same proportion of children from working-class families obtained grammar school places as they had two decades prior to the Act. Income, occupation, family size and parental education were still associated with rates of grammar school entry and drop out and the likelihood of leaving school early and under-qualified.

The corollary was that that the 1944 Act conferred on the middle classes all the advantages they had enjoyed in the pre-war years. Their children were over-represented in and continued to benefit from highly esteemed schools which, in turn, led to public examinations and the credentials that cashed out in the entry to higher education and clerical, managerial and professional employment. Secondary schooling, therefore, reflected and reproduced broad divisions within the occupational structure and between social classes. The research demonstrated that access, opportunity and success in secondary education were closely associated with patterns of income, occupational status, family arrangements and family size. Official reports, such as *Early Leaving*, also began to identify family and community values and cultures as causal factors in the explanation of differential access, staying on rates and attainment. They did not dwell on issues such as gulfs in funding on buildings and equipment, teaching materials and salaries that existed between grammar and secondary modern schools. A vocabulary with which pedagogic processes that largely formed, then accepted or rejected different class and gender activities had, in Bernstein's terms, 'yet to be thought'. Its discourse truly was a relay for other, dominant voices.

The intellectual field of the sociology of education, as represented in these studies, drew attention primarily to social class patterns of shifting educational achievement and relative failure. In practice, the basis of analysis was occupational groupings rather than any well developed sense of social class. Documenting the social justice implications of selective secondary education was probably one of sociology of education's most significant contributions. Its foundational years demonstrating the extent to which it could contribute to public policy debates and to larger social science themes, most notably in measuring and understanding social mobility. It remains one of the discipline's finest moments, despite its silences, in retrospect, amounting to bias, on issues, such as gender and constituted much of the reason why researchers, including the authors, pursued it as a field of study.

4 Comprehensive schooling
Challenging inequality?

Introduction

British secondary education since the mid-1970s has been largely based on comprehensive schools that are intended to provide for children of all abilities. In purpose and function they appear to stand in stark contrast to the system we described in the previous two chapters that primarily focused on the identification of a relatively small group of academically able students with the ability to benefit from the superior resourcing of a selective grammar school education, while the great majority were allocated to secondary modern schools and limited prospects in the labour market. The scope of the change over the past 40 years has been considerable, though uneven in pace and coverage across the four British 'home nations'. In Wales and Scotland today there are no grammar schools and the fee-paying sector is very small. Approximately 95 per cent of secondary school students in Scotland and over 98 per cent of their counterparts in Wales are in comprehensives. In England in 2003 (DfES, 2003) 4 per cent of secondary age students attended the remaining 163 grammar schools and about 9 per cent were enrolled in fee-paying schools so that, at face value, 87 per cent of students in England attended comprehensive schools. Alternatively, we might say that only about one-third of the proportion of the age group who were in overtly selective schools in the 1960s now attend them. However, as we shall see, there were and are considerable intake differences between comprehensive schools. In contrast Northern Ireland retains selective education, based largely on a system of sectarian grammar and state comprehensive schools.

There are two questions that we will address in this chapter. The first concerns what drove the transformation and why the system has assumed the character it now has. The second broader question relates to issues of educational reproduction; has the system opened up opportunities for social mobility via education previously unavailable under the selective system?

Going comprehensive from the ground up

If the scale of change from a system based on selective education to one predominantly based on comprehensive schools is remarkable, for policy scholars its trajectory provides a unique opportunity to analyse change that began on the ground. It has been a process within which the conventional sequences of policy formation and transmission, from production or contextualisation to recontextualisation and reproduction, have not applied in any straightforward way. This was not a policy formulated at the centre and implemented locally, rather the reverse. The pluralistic character of British education in the 20 years following the 1944 Education Act provided the social and educational contexts within which transformation from selective to comprehensive education took place.

At the level of ideas, there are two historical aspects of comprehensive education that must be grasped. First, there were those, including many in the pre-war teacher associations, for whom the expansion of secondary education was to take place within a system of multilateral, or all-ability schools (Simon and Rubenstein, 1969). For them, advocating radical reform of schooling, what emerged in the 1944 Act was a bitter disappointment. Second, others adopted an approach that was both principled and pragmatic but primarily oppositional in character, where comprehensive schools were seen as a way out of the manifest injustices of selective education. In opposition to such selective education, educational administrators, including key LEA officers, teachers and parents coalesced in local groups to argue for comprehensive schools (Pedley, 1974; Kerckhoff *et al.*, 1996; Simon and Rubenstein, 1969). Unfortunately, knowing what one was up against did not guarantee clear focus on what one was aiming for. Exactly what comprehensive schools should look like in curriculum and pedagogic terms was not worked through with any degree of precision. Quite how schools were to teach children with a 'comprehensive' or full range of educational capabilities was imperfectly thought through, as was the thorny issue of admissions policies. How was it to be ensured that comprehensives were, indeed, 'comprehensive'? The answers to these questions were pragmatically assembled, in local circumstances, as policy unfolded across the UK.

The local nature of alliances that arose in pursuit of comprehensive education lay in the structure of governance of British education and in successive central governments' commitment to selective education. We noted in earlier chapters that the Labour government 1945–51 put its support behind selection and central government policy was avowedly anti-comprehensive for a full decade after 1944. Only between 1958–64 did it reluctantly begin to accept what was emerging at the grass roots,. The movement was local because LEAs were responsible for the organisation of education within their administrative boundaries. Comprehensive education had to advance on an LEA by LEA basis in the absence of any central directive for change. While they enjoyed considerable autonomy from central government, each had to secure the agreement of Ministers and their officials to any major changes in provision if this involved significant alteration in the way central government grants to LEAs were utilised. Central government, therefore, retained considerable powers to regulate the pace and direction of change and, indeed, up until 1965 it did that in respect of comprehensive schools.

For Kerckhoff *et al.* (1996) the evolution of comprehensive education went through two distinct phases in the immediate post-1944 period: 1945–51 when comprehensives were overlooked; and 1951–64 when 'cautious experimentation', developed in reaction to the perceived effects of selective education. There was much to be uneasy about, as we suggested in the previous chapters. Concerns about 'early leaving' or 'wastage' were expressed in England and Scotland. In Scotland in 1949, for example, of the students allocated to selective secondary schools, two-thirds (67 per cent) had left without qualifications by the beginning of their fifth year (Gray *et al.*, 1983). Dale and Griffith (1965) conducted a study in a single Welsh grammar school where over 40 per cent of the age cohort entered that identified those pupils who 'improved' or 'deteriorated' in the first year (defined by falling or rising through its streams), finding over a five-year period that the former were overwhelmingly from working-class backgrounds and the latter were from middle-class backgrounds. In their view, in only two of the cases of 39 deteriorators was lack of intellectual ability its main cause. Patterns of 'staying on' and O level performance correlated much more highly with end of first year results than 'scholarship exam' rank orders, hardly a good argument for the beneficial effects of selective education and social mobility.

The first steps towards the creation of comprehensive education appeared in Anglesea, London, Middlesex, Coventry, Oldham and West Riding (Pedley, 1974). Their establishment demonstrated the uneasy relation between central government and LEAs when it came to moving away from selective education. When Kidbrooke, the first purpose-built comprehensive secondary school, opened in 1954 in South London, the Minister of Education, Florence Horsborough, refused to allow the closure of the nearby Eltham Hill Girls' Grammar School and prevented its students being transferred to Kidbrooke. The co-existence of the two schools meant that Kidbrooke could not become fully 'comprehensive' because its intake was 'creamed' by Eltham Hill (Pedley, 1974). In 1955, in a similar vein, Manchester was prevented from developing two new comprehensives, although a third was allowed to open because it was not a 'new build' scheme.

In regulating the development of comprehensive schools in the period 1954–8, the Ministry applied a set of principles that governed the pace of change. It became clear that it would not support the closure of existing grammar schools, nor would it grant permission for comprehensives to be built adjacent to them, thus challenging existing selective arrangements. It did allow existing secondary moderns to be redesignated comprehensive. In effect, new comprehensives were mainly located on green field sites on the periphery of urban areas and provided schooling, initially, for council estate and new occupier development on the outskirts of towns and cities. Moreover, it was intended that these new schools should educate pupils aged 11–18, so that they were required to have post-compulsory Sixth Forms. In order to provide a full range of subjects at A level, however, these had to be large and, to ensure that they could be sustained, the new comprehensives also had to be large, with intakes of over 1500 students. The majority of secondaries in the UK were smaller, 700–800 students constituting a large school (Pedley, 1974: Simon and Rubenstein, 1969). The perception that 'comprehensive' equalled 'large and impersonal' was an image that was to persist for some decades after their establishment.

Although progress was uneven and halting, some LEAs pursued comprehensive education with vigour. By 1958, the London County Council had opened 26 comprehensives for 11–18-year-olds (Kerckhoff *et al.*, 1996) while, elsewhere, the 'breakout' from selective education took a different form. Leicestershire proposed an 'experiment' in non-selective education in 1957, setting out a plan for a two-tier system involving high and upper schools, with transfers at 11 and 14 (Kerckhoff *et al.*, 1996) which claimed several advantages. It avoided 11–18, all-through secondary schools and the problem of size stemming from the requirement to support a Sixth Form. Existing secondaries were only required to be redesignated rather than closed or amalgamated to achieve a non-selective system. Former secondary moderns became 11–14 high schools and lost their stigmatised status while existing grammar schools, re-designated as upper schools, retained their close relation with the preparation of students for public examinations and the expertise of their staff was not lost to the system (Kerckhoff *et al.*, 1996). The wider significance was that it provided another model with which LEAs might think through the reorganisation of secondary education, away from dominant, selective arrangements. Although they may have been attractive, the two-tier models of secondary provision were not widely adopted.

By 1960, with minimal support from central government, there were 130 comprehensive schools in England and Wales, their numbers doubling to 262 by 1965, providing for 8.5 per cent of the secondary school population (Kerckhoff *et al.*, 1996). Not all of the schools had fully comprehensive intakes. In Coventry, for example, two direct grant grammar schools and one maintained girls' grammar creamed off the most able students throughout the city (Simon and Rubenstein, 1969). This was true of other large towns and cities, such that Simon and Rubenstein contended that the most genuine comprehensive schools, admitting the full range of abilities, were likely to be found in rural, county areas of England and Wales. By 1962 Wales had 22 comprehensives, mainly in the rural North and West. Progress was slower in the urbanised Southeast because central governments continued to insist on diversity and the retention of grammar schools. In Scotland, Glasgow had opened 22 comprehensives by 1962 (Simon and Rubenstein, 1969).

What was driving the change?

In their study of the evolution of the comprehensive school, Simon and Rubenstein (1969) suggested five factors underlying decisions to change from selective to comprehensive education:

1   technological change and economic advance. Technological change reduced demand for unskilled workers and increased it for those with specialised skills and adaptability. Contemporary official reports, such as the Crowther Report (1959) noted the need for a more educated, adaptable and skilled workforce, whose expansion, some thought, grammar schools functionally limited;

2   changes in secondary modern schools. Until 1951 secondary modern schools were not allowed to enter students for public exams, such as the School Certificate (which from 1954 became GCE O levels, generally taken at the age of 16). This restriction was lifted and by 1953 secondary modern school students demonstrated they could sit and pass exams formerly reserved for their grammar school counterparts. The numbers were never large, only one in eight of their students recording GCE successes in 1960 but their existence cast further doubt on the validity of selection at 11+, demonstrating its wastefulness and inefficiency in developing taken;

3   parental aspiration. Contemporary surveys suggested that when parents were asked what kind of secondary education they would like for their sons and daughters, over 50 per cent stated a preference for grammar schools, 20 per cent chose technical schools, while only 16 per cent chose secondary moderns. In Nottingham in 1954 there were 447 places for approximately 4,400 children, schools selecting about 1,300 to go for the 'scholarship' exam, while parents insisted that another 1,400 be entered. In all 2,716 children competed for 447 places, of whom 2,269 'failed', presumably mainly those entered at the behest of parents. It is argued that such disappointment fed through into local pressure for change;

4   social class and opportunity. Academic research and official reports, such as *Early Leaving* stripped away any pretensions that selective education was socially just and gave ammunition to politicians, administrators, teachers and parents calling for reform; and

5   the critique of segregation. By the mid-1950s psychologists' critique of IQ was complemented by their critical look at the impact of segregation on children of different educational capabilities in different schools. Vernon and others argued that the IQs of boys aged 14 attending grammar and technical schools tended to rise, while they fell for students in secondary moderns, further evidence that selective education was not entirely beneficial as a system.

While all of these were clearly important as underlying explanations in constituting a discourse increasingly shared by those seeking extension of comprehensive education, there were also demographic, personal and party political influences at work. First, demographic change in the form of the baby boom and the formation of new families in the postwar period gave rise to the growth of estates and new towns on the periphery of existing cities and conurbations, particularly in the North, Midlands and South East of England. These, in turn, required new schools, providing opportunity for LEAs to think and build differently, with less interference from central government. Second, there were outstanding educational administrators who, with the support of local government elected members, were able to envision and realise something other than conventional, selective education. Chief Education Officers Stuart Mason (Leicestershire) and Alex Clegg (West Riding) were notable examples. From 1958 onward their task was made easier by a more sympathetic view of comprehensive schools by Education Ministers in Conservative governments. They and their officials took increasingly less obstructive stances toward changes taking place on the ground primarily, though not exclusively, in Labour controlled authorities. Edward Boyle, who took office in 1962, embraced the idea of comprehensive education, although many others in his Conservative Party did not, and exercised his powers, when possible, to facilitate LEA plans to move away from selective education (Simon and Rubenstein, 1969). In 1963, he used a party political TV broadcast to announce that LEA plans would be considered strictly on their educational merit and not on the political complexion of the authority and many took this as encouragement to submit those which introduced comprehensive schools (Kerckhoff *et al.*, 1996). Civil servants estimated that by 1963 the majority of LEAs had either submitted or were developing plans for reorganisation. By this time, movement at the grass roots had fundamentally altered the organisation of education in England, Wales and Scotland.

With the accession of a Labour Government in 1964, the expectation was that comprehensive secondary education would become government policy. That expectation was met when Anthony Crosland, their Education Secretary issued what was called Circular 10/65, which famously 'requested' rather than required LEAs to submit plans, within a year, for reorganisation on comprehensive lines. No single pattern was laid down, although six possible models were identified, and these embraced both single and two-tier modes of organisation.

10/65 and after: comprehensive schooling and its challenges

After 10/65 the policy framework changed, with comprehensive schooling actively encouraged by central government. Table 4.1 tells the story of the rapid growth in comprehensive provision between 1965–70. By 1973 just half of the secondary school population were enrolled in Comprehensive Schools, Margaret Thatcher, who assumed office as Education Secretary in 1970 in Edward Heath's Conservative government, having been required to approve plans submitted by LEAs which progressively rolled back selective education. To her discomfort when she was Prime Minister after 1979, opposition politicians reminded her that she had been responsible for the closure of more grammar schools than any other Education Secretary before or since her period in office.

Table 4.1 Growth of comprehensive schooling 1965–70

Year	No. of schools	% of secondary school population
1965	262	8.5
1966	387	11.1
1967	507	14.4
1968	748	20.9
1969	960	26.0
1970	1,145	31.0

Source: Simon and Rubenstein, 1969: 109.

Support for comprehensive education was far from unanimous, especially by groups who felt they threatened standards in education best represented by grammar schools. Circular 10/65 provoked the creation of the National Education Association, the first of many organisations devoted to the preservation of grammar schools and opposition of comprehensive education (Benn and Chitty, 1966; Kerckhoff *et al.*, 1996). A number of others (e.g. Hillgate, The Freedom Association) and a succession of right wing secondary school media pundits (e.g. Rhodes Boyson, the headteacher of grammar turned comprehensive, Highbury Boys) predicted that the demise of grammar schools would bring to an end civilisation, as they knew it. Opposition to comprehensive schools was amplified by publications known as the *Black Papers* (Cox and Dyson, 1969; Cox, 1981) in which a coalition of Tory politicians, academics and journalists wrote highly critical commentaries about comprehensive schools around which negative media reporting coalesced. Benn and Chitty (1996) claimed that commentary was narrowly based and sectarian, rather than broadly based and emanating from the grass roots. A long-term consequence has been that supporters of comprehensive education, including organisations like the Campaign for the Advancement of State Education (CASE), became inured to defensiveness in promoting non-selective forms of schooling. Its objectors provided ideological ground on which some LEAs, like Bexley, managed to preserve overtly selective education and others have more recently expanded it afresh. One way or another selective education has remained a bedrock policy within national Conservative party politics, even if this has not always been a view shared by all Conservative dominated LEAs while Labour, back in office after 1997, as we shall see in Chapter 8, have indulged more in the politics of gesture than action with respect of selection.

Given that comprehensive secondary schools have eventually become the dominant but not universal form of secondary provision, particularly in England, to what extent have they provided the experience of 'common schooling'? The answer would have to be that it was not as much as was anticipated by some of their early advocates, who saw them as social melting pots. As comprehensive schools developed two broad issues had to be addressed. The first related to the requirement that, like their primary school counterparts, they existed for students of all abilities. How was their progress to be accomplished effectively and efficiently? The second related to school admissions. How was it to be decided as to who went where? Did neighbourhoods rule? Whether ability intakes were to be balanced had considerable bearing on patterns of educational reproduction.

Provision for students across the ability range could vary markedly between adjacent schools in the same LEA, just as the character of the ability intakes available to different schools could vary widely. In narrative terms, from the outset comprehensive schools adopted policies that broadly placed children with different abilities, however these were measured, in different classes for teaching purposes. Benn and Simons's *Half Way There*, published in 1972, surveyed over 1,400 schools and reported that in 1968, 88 per cent of comprehensive schools employed some form of streaming, banding, setting or other possible combination. Streaming, as we use the term here, referred to a form of pupil grouping where a cohort of students was differentiated in terms of a particular criterion, such as an IQ or, more usually, language and/or maths ability and individuals placed with like-minded others in teaching groups that remained the same for all subjects. Schools often divided pupils into three broad 'bands' of ability on the same criteria. Setting referred to practices where ability grouping changed subject by subject, depending upon prior attainment. A child might be in the top set group for one subject, but middle or lower ranking ones in others. This was regarded as more flexible in recognising the variety of talents that students might possess. Students might end up in a variety of differently composed groups.

By 1971, Benn and Simon recorded that the population of students in their survey of comprehensives who were taught in streams had fallen from 19.5 to 4.5 per cent, while those in broad ability bands had increased from 31 to 45 per cent, and various forms mixed ability classes accounted for 34.6 per cent of students (Benn and Simon, 1972: 219). On the evidence of work carried out a few years later by the authors (Davies, 1977; Corbishley, 1977; Evans, 1985) such data must be regarded as very rough-hewn. Schools employed complex combinations of these modes, often varying across subjects and year groups and knew of and reported upon them somewhat imperfectly. When schools in Greater London 'went mixed ability' as they had in large numbers by the mid-1970s, they did so for a variety of motives, predominantly 'technicist', that is, as their response to the often very wide range of primary schools and practices that their intakes had previously encountered and the poor quality of information that they claimed accompanied them on their move to secondary. Homogeneously grouping their 'first years' constituted a wiping of the slate clean, an election to rely on their own means of diagnosing student ability rather than those of a variety of their primary 'feeders'. We referred to it as 'Red Riding Hood' mixed ability – all the better to set them with later. It was least likely to extend to modern languages and maths and tapered off in second and third years to become a practice only fallen back on when numbers choosing a subject in the four and fifth years were too small to justify an alternative. A few others tried mixed ability as a marketing ploy, attempting to signal that their 'difference' was that they took this business of 'diagnosis' seriously, while even fewer adopted it on what could be called 'egalitarian' grounds, sustaining it across all subjects for the first three years and allowing it as far as seemed feasible thereafter, signifying a determination to search for a new pedagogic discourse that would seek appropriate curricular and transmission modes for children of all abilities who ought to learn together.

These differences in motives and meanings tended to matter a great deal both as to how long mixed ability forms were persevered with, how completely they were organised, that is, how far low ability/poorly behaving students were 'extracted' and what form 'within classroom' grouping took, across what range of the curriculum, as well as how diligently and successfully effort was expended on appropriate curricular and classroom work practices and inservice teacher education that reskilled participants in their use and preparation. Death by a thousand nonindividuated worksheets became the fate of approximately a school generation until curriculum reshapers within the PRF caught up with the production of wide-ability friendly materials that permitted legitimate variation of pacing across more loosely classified contents (Evans, 1985). In their follow up study conducted in 1993–4, Benn and Chitty (1996: 258) reported that in Year 8 (the second year of secondary school, at age 12), forms of streaming operated in only 1.5 per cent of schools, banding in 9 per cent and setting in 16 per cent, the rest employing various forms of mixed ability grouping (74 per cent) that had 'gradually become naturalised into routine practice in many schools'. It diminished sharply thereafter to become unusual from Year 10 (the fourth year). One presumes that the percentages for streaming and setting referred to 'exclusively so' while that for mixed ability grouping indicated a 'more or less' presence.

In placing students of different abilities in different classrooms have we replicated a key characteristic of selective systems? Any answer must be equivocal; children are not allocated to different schools and opportunities exist to share a common ethos within a common school. However, on the evidence of Gamoran (1987) and his Chicago colleagues on the effects of 'tracking' in city schools in the USA, 'children going to the same building may only in a limited sense be attending the same school' (Davies and Evans, 2001). It is very likely that children who are placed in groups according to ability, however it is measured, will experience a shared school very differently. Children in the more academic streams can, and do, face both opportunities and pressures that are different from those experienced in the classes where academic expectations are less intense (Daniels and Creese, 2004; Arnot and Reay, 2004).

Jo Boaler's study of maths teaching in two schools which practised a variety of pupil grouping strategies can be taken as a particularly well-worked, recent reminder of how differentiation in comprehensive settings can be experienced by students and teachers (Boaler, 1997). It focused on how pupils were grouped for maths teaching in two secondary comprehensive schools. Amber Hill had first year mixed ability classes while, in the second year, pupils were placed in sets but paced their own work via extensive use of individual work books. For the last three years of compulsory education, 14–16-year-old pupils remained in sets but the pace of learning was strongly teacher determined. At Phoenix Park, the second school in the study, mathematics was taught wholly in mixed-ability settings, in classrooms where students worked collaboratively on projects that asked 'big questions'. Only at the last possible moment, in the last term prior to the GCSE exam at age 16 were students placed in 'tiered groups' that broadly matched the 'tiered' examination papers that they would be required to sit. The investigation included bench-marking tests specifically constructed for the study and given to students in their first year. It was, therefore, possible to 'model' or devise predictions about expected outcomes in terms of examination achievements for students, thereby making it possible to compare schools and the effectiveness of teaching in setted and non-setted classrooms.

Boaler's research confirmed aspects of the findings of a variety of earlier studies (e.g. Ford, 1969; Edwards *et al.*, 1989) that pupil grouping by ability aligned educational and social selection or, quite simply, that more academic groups are also more middle class in origin. Being in a 'top' set had a deleterious effect on some students, especially girls. The pace of lessons, high expectations and pressure to keep up led to what Boaler called 'survival of the quickest'. Being restricted to sitting papers from which they could gain no more than a 'C' grade led to the disaffection of less talented students in other sets. Overall, she concluded that fewer students matched the attainment levels projected from their entry-level test results than students at Phoenix Park, where mixed ability with collaborative pedagogies enabled the majority of students to meet or exceed their predicted grades across social class and gender categories.

Boaler's findings are important and the rigour of the design and its application ensure that her findings are likely to be secure. But do larger scale studies of student grouping tell us anything different? The most extensive, large-scale British study of pupil grouping in recent years was that by Hallam, Ireson and Hurley (Ireson and Hallam, 2001; Ireson *et al.*, 2002) who investigated the effects of pupil grouping in English, maths and science in Years 7–9 (the first three, when students are 11–13) in 45 secondary schools in the UK. Of the 45 schools, 15 operated mixed ability classrooms in all subjects, 15 combined mixed ability with some setting and 15 schools were organised around streaming or banding. They collected information on 1,500 teachers and over 6,000 students, including national assessment performance at KS2 (where the students are in the last year of primary school), KS3 (at age 14) and, later, KS4 results at age 16+.

Their findings suggested that the impact of pupil grouping was by no means straightforward. It was difficult to ascertain any overall impact of pupil groups because effects varied from subject to subject. The amount of time students spent in setted or non-setted classrooms did not appear to have any great effect at KS3 in English or science but did in maths. Set placement, however, did appear to have an effect at KS3 and KS4. Broadly, able students placed in 'high' maths sets progressed further, while low sets had a deleterious effect on students who made less progress than students in middle and upper ability groups. The least able children benefited most and made better progress in mixed ability settings. It was argued that much of the effect of grouping strategies is mediated by students' 'self-concept'. Where this was supported and enhanced progress was likely to be better and vice versa. In part, this was held to account for the differential progress made by middle and least-able children in mixed ability settings. Much also depended on how grouping arrangements worked in individual schools, so that it is possible that the effect of the same kind of ability grouping was to achieve slightly different outcomes, school by school. Overall, the study gave little comfort either to advocates of streaming, setting or to those convinced of the efficacy of mixed ability classrooms. It was assumed that more thought had to be given to the specific forms of curriculum content and pedagogy associated with particular subjects. It might well be that subjects or classrooms where knowledge is taught and assessed in logical, hierarchical, series of steps, where 'mastery' of one stage is thought to be necessary before proceeding to the next, align more with setting than those where pedagogy is not constructed in this way. The authors also suggested that more thought ought to be given to within-class grouping so that a better 'fit' may be found between content, pacing and aptitude, at the same time encouraging collaboration.

A further, relevant study, built upon Boaler's earlier work, focused primarily on pupil grouping in maths classes (Wiliam and Bartholomew, 2004), sampling 955 pupils from six secondary comprehensive schools to investigate the effect of grouping on student performance as they progressed form KS3 (at age 14) to their GCSE examinations (at age 16). Assessment performance data at GCSE stage was gathered and set against pupils' experience of grouping gathered via survey, interview and observation data about teaching styles and learners' experiences collected via 150 lesson observations. All students claimed to have experience of setted classes, although length of time spent in sets varied substantially across schools. One school placed students in sets as early as Year 8, three at the beginning of Year 9 and the remainder at the beginning of Year 10. Setting procedures varied by school, condensed into a 4-fold classification of 'top', 'upper', 'lower' and 'bottom'. As in Boaler's study, KS3 assessments, and maths examinations at GCSE were 'tiered', so that only those doing the 'top tier' or most difficult paper could achieve a grade above C. Tiering also operated punitively, so that students doing the top tier paper who failed to gain C grade, received only the lowest grade G. Allocation of students to sets, then, provide the means of preparing students for different examination papers fraught with such considerations.

The study confirmed what has been reported elsewhere over the last two decades; working-class students were more likely to be allocated to lower sets than their middle-class counterparts with similar scores, more so in some schools than others, the most notable example being the school with a predominately middle-class intake. Overall, KS3 results operated as good predictions of what grades were achieved at GCSE and, with minor exceptions, progress made by students at each of the schools was more similar than different. However, there were reported advantages to being placed in the top set where students, on average, achieved half a grade better than predicted on the basis of KS3 scores. Students of bottom sets achieved half a grade lower than would be expected. Wiliam and Bartholomew (2004) concluded that it:

> does show that the set into which you are allocated – an allocation over which students have little, if any, influence at any of the six schools – makes a huge difference to how well you do, and much more of a difference than schools which you go to.
>
> (Wiliam and Bartholomew, 2004: 288)

The overall effect of setting, however, they argued, was not to raise levels of achievement. If anything it depressed them slightly and, as with previous research, the chief beneficiaries of setting in maths were higher achieving students and those who gained least are lower attaining students, producing an increase in the spread of achievement within the cohort. For Wiliam and Bartholomew, how setting gave rise to these outcomes requires us to consider the interaction between grouping pupils of similar attainment and the kinds of teaching that takes place in sets. Building on Boaler (2000), they argue that sets encourage the perception that all students in a classroom are of similar ability, such that pedagogically important differences between individuals and subsets tend to be overlooked. Moreover, students in lower sets who tended to be taught by least qualified teachers, experienced a narrower range of teaching strategies and found their requests for more challenging work ignored by teachers whose expectations aligned with their low set status. More or less the opposite pertained in top sets where, if anything, pacing tended to be too fast for many students, especially girls. Mixed ability classes were more likely to receive a wide range of teaching strategies, with greater attention paid to individual differences. The field appears to be on the verge of discovering or taking seriously what Bernstein contended in 1971; like love and marriage, decisions about pedagogy – content, methods, evaluation, grouping and the forms of social relation that they engender not only 'go together' but change in the modality of one involves change (or else creates dissonance) in others.

Some early advocates of comprehensive schooling have seen it as a means of avoiding early selection and differentiation. They also see mixed ability grouping as a necessary corollary in rooting out the generative principles of a divided system of education though most early research in this somewhat complicated area was a triumph of enthusiasm over insight, with a systematic tendency to produce findings at odds with current, dominant practice (Corbishley, 1977). Recent research, as Boaler and Wiliam and Bartholomew demonstrate, suggests that schools operate very different pupil-grouping policies and that the majority of children in comprehensives experience both mixed ability environments and more homogeneous pupil grouping by attainment.

As with any other secondary mode, like their broad-ability primary precursors, comprehensive schools reproduce and project social class divisions that exist outside as they inevitably select inside. Setting produces hierarchies of talent that are socially stratified by class, as well as by gender and ethnicity which build on advantages and disadvantages brought into the education system. The hope for many has been that comprehensive schools allow greater flexibility in ability grouping practices and the possibility of paying greater attention to individual aptitudes on a subject by subject basis in pursuing equity. Some of the research findings presented above suggest that this is not just a forlorn hope. However, arranging pedagogic practice so that it favours the lowly ranked seems at odds with much of our policy and practice which suggests that early differentiation by educational experience and labour market destinies projected by a divided system are infinitely more preferable to the majority of the socially powerful.

Neighbourhoods and differentiation between schools

There are a number of ways by which divided education systems can be achieved. Selection by psychometric and attainment measures, as for grammar and secondary modern schools was one, legally based racially segregated schooling, as existed in the USA until overturned by Brown versus Board of Education in 1954 was another. These invidiously stratifying systems have now largely been replaced in Britain by a third principle, what we might call 'selection by mortgage' (see Gorard *et al.*, 2003). In the broadest sense, it means that different schools achieve differentiated ability and socio-economic intakes because they reflect the neighbourhoods or 'catchment areas' in which they are located and serve. In this section we discuss why this might be important when we consider comprehensive education and educational reproduction.

From the beginning, as we noted, there has been an interest in the relationship between comprehensive schools and location (Ford, 1969; Simon and Rubenstein, 1969; Bellaby, 1977; Shaw, 1983; Benn and Chitty, 1996; Taylor, 2002). The concern arose in consideration of the extent to which the geographical assignment of children to schools would or could lead to the creation of schools that were 'comprehensive' in the sense of having a range and balance of students by social class and levels of attainment. It was certainly the intention of central government after 1965 that they should be rendered explicit in Circular 10/65 which urged '[Local Education] authorities to ensure, when determining catchment areas, that schools are as socially and intellectually comprehensive as is practicable' (cited in Shaw, 1983: 66). The devil, as always, was in the detail of what constituted 'practicable'. Since their establishment, assignment of children to schools other than selective and church-affiliated has tended to be on the basis of the geographic proximity of their homes. The rationale for the almost universal use of geographically immediate 'catchment areas' as a means of such allocation was fairly straightforward. They were simple to administer, offered LEAs a transparent and ostensibly fair mechanism to allocate students to places and allowed children to travel the shortest distance to school. Bussing has been anathema in ensuring 'balanced' comprehensive intakes while being the lifeblood of special and Welsh medium education and, without extensive daily travel, selective and church schools could not fill their places. Historically, therefore, it has been more or less impossible to ensure that schools should be socially and intellectually mixed via the use of 'nearest to school' catchment areas.

In the 1950s and 1960s there were two hurdles. The continued existence of maintained and direct grant grammar schools meant that they 'creamed' the newly established comprehensives Moreover, many of the newer schools, as we noted earlier, were located on the periphery of urban centres, often near postwar council estates that attracted few or no old middle and professional class families. One example of how this worked in the 1950s and 1960s was in Coventry, where Woodlands and Couldon Castle schools were created as 1,500+ comprehensives built on the edge of the city. However, primary school children throughout Coventry, including those in their catchment areas, sat the 11+ to gain entry into either direct grant grammar or maintained girls grammar schools (Simon and Rubenstein, 1969). While Woodlands and Couldon Castle served both council estates and new owner-occupier estates on the city's periphery, children of professional and old middle-class families were largely absent from them. This was, and continues to be, a widely repeated British pattern.

Although grammar schools have disappeared from Wales and Scotland, and from many parts of England, the aim of achieving comprehensive schools that are homogeneously socially and educationally mixed has not been realised. Schools remain socially and educationally segregated now, as in the past, although the stratification system has changed somewhat. We can illustrate our point by drawing on recent research on the relationship between school composition and school performance (Gorard *et al.*, 2003).

Table 4.2 shows the proportion of children eligible for free school meals (FSM) in a large urban centre in South East Wales. We have assigned each school a letter. FSM is a widely accepted indicator of levels of student family poverty. Moreover, FSM remain a very good inverse predictor of school performance, as measured, say by the proportion of 16-years-olds obtaining GCSE grades A★–C. Furthermore, Gorard (2000) and Gorard *et al.* (2003) show that patterns and principles derived from Wales apply equally in England.

Table 4.2 shows considerable segregation between, say, school C where about 5 per cent of children are eligible for FSM compared with 55 per cent at school M. In School C, over 70 per cent of students achieve GCSE grades A★–C, while only about 12 per cent do so in school M. These patterns, both in school composition and school performance have been stable over the last 15 years. So, what is driving the segregation? The answer is primarily the housing market and its interaction with secondary schools. Secondary school admissions in this city have been based on a system of 'feeder' primary schools, attendance at which determines secondary school allocation. Exceptions are made for some categories of new applicants, such as allowing siblings to attend the same school but geographical proximity is the primary mechanism shaping school admissions. Housing, historically has been segregated, by price and by forms of ownership (council/owner-occupier) and is reflected, where catchment areas operate, in the social composition of schools. Housing markets both sustain and interact with school reputations and, in so doing, sustain segregation. This explains the polarisation between schools C and M. School C is an ex-grammar school located

Table 4.2 The proportion of children entitled to free school meals in LEA secondary schools in a Welsh Urban Centre, 2003

School	% students entitled to FSM 2003	School	% students entitled to FSM 2003
A	37.81	H	12.34
B	48.12	I	11.66
C	5.17	J	43.34
D	16.39	K	34.95
E	44.45	L	6.88
F	31.68	M	55.11
G	31.03		

Note
City average 25.57.

in an area of expensive suburban housing but it also has in its catchment an inner urban area that contain academic families employed at the nearby university. The historic reputation of the school and the housing market have interacted to put a 'premium' on house prices in the catchment. School M is located near both peripheral housing and owner-occupier estates. The Welsh Inspectorate deemed it a 'failing school' in its first inspection. It has been renamed and with the support of the LEA has been given a 'fresh start'. Its results continue to reflect its intake and it has lost even more pupils to adjacent schools on its side of the city. There are planned LEA changes in admissions policies but it is unlikely these will significantly alter the prevailing pattern of segregation in the city. Changing the school mix, within the limits set by church and Welsh medium intakes, could be achieved via bussing but the public and political will to bring that about does not exist.

Comprehensive education can and does separate children by social class. As we shall argue in more detail in later chapters it has not proved to be the solvent of social stratification to the degree some of its advocates had hoped. That, however, should not obscure the immense changes to which comprehensive schools have made a decisive contribution. In their praise, Sally Tomlinson (2004, p. 4), eloquently noted that:

> standards, as measured by those entered for and passing public examinations have been steadily rising since the 1960s. In 1962, when some 20% were selected for grammar schools, 16% of pupils obtained five O level passes. In 2000/1 51% achieved the equivalent five GCSE passes. The A level exam – originally designed for less than 10% of pupils, was achieved in two or more subjects) by 37% of pupils in 2001. In 1970, 47% left school without any qualifications – by 2000 this had fallen to 10%. In the early 1960s some 10% of young people went on to higher education. The Robbins Committee (1963) recommended an increase to 17%. Now around 40% are in higher education and there is a laudable aim of increasing this to 50%. Those who persist in asserting that more working class children made it into higher education when grammar schools were the norm should revisit the Robbins Report. Their survey in 1961/2 showed that 64% of students in HE at that time had fathers in professional or managerial jobs, only 4% had fathers in semiskilled jobs and only 2% came from unskilled parentage.
>
> (*Robbins Report*, 1963: 50)

In terms of raising the volume of students moving through compulsory education and then going on to achieve a considerable measure of success in public examinations, it can be claimed that comprehensive schools have been successful. Moreover, in relation to fee-paying, grammar, grant maintained, church and specialist schools, the results that comprehensives achieve, as measured by public examination, are on a par when we take into account their social composition. It is worthwhile recalling that the background characteristics of students account for about 80 per cent of the total variance of school outcomes (Gorard *et al.*,

2003) and that the proportion of children on FSM alone will account for about 70 per cent. In short, schools with a high proportion of children on FSM are likely to achieve poorer results than schools with a small proportion of FSM children. As we show in detail in Chapter 8, voluntary-aided (VA) and controlled schools, faith schools and foundation schools have far more 'privileged intakes' than their LEA counterparts (Gorard, 2000; Gorard and Taylor, 2001). However it can also be shown that while a 'gap' exists between the 49.4 per cent of children in faith-based schools obtaining more than 5 GCSE's A*–C in 1997 compared with 42.3 per cent doing so in other schools (most of which was accounted for by differences in school composition), the gap had closed slightly by 2001. We will discuss performance differences between LEA comprehensives and other kinds of secondary schools in more detail in the next chapter.

Conclusion

Comprehensive education developed from the bottom up to the extent that central government was forced to change from resisting to embracing it in 1965. It began and proceeded in the early years primarily as a programme to roll back selective education. It can be argued that there were diverse justifications for its introduction, over time various arguments receiving various kinds of emphasis among its protagonists. It was and remains a policy vulnerable to 'standards' arguments promoted by those who see grammar schools as the last bastions for the preservation of a culture and tradition associated with curricular and pedagogic styles generated to educate the elite few. Moreover, the idea of the 'common school' ideal in comprehensive education is increasingly under threat from policies designed to promote 'choice and diversity' in state education. This will be discussed in more detail in Chapters 7 and 8.

Comprehensive education has generated heterogeneous experiences for students both between and within schools. Old visions where projected placement in the labour market was largely determined at the age of 11 have disappeared to be replaced by a more diffuse kind of segregation by mortgage. How and to what extent the school you attend, in comprehensive systems, influences the results you achieve, however, is by no means clear-cut. School mix, that is, the social and intellectual composition of schools, may have very little direct impact. What does matter, however, according to the research we have reported here, are grouping practices and their interaction with pedagogic choices of tactic, such as may make a grade different at age 16 for one in four students (Wiliam and Bartholomew, 2004). Although, comprehensive schools have removed the old stigma of 'failure' at 11 and have promoted perceptions that opportunities for education progress exist for a wider range of students up to and beyond compulsory schooling learning age. The development of comprehensive schooling has coincided with a huge expansion in the number of children staying on at school and continuing in education after the age of compulsory schooling and a large increase in the number of students obtaining educational qualifications that are recognised in the job market. To what extent, though, has this reversed the associations between selective education and patterns of entry to the labour market? Do children from all social backgrounds compete for the most desirable jobs? Have the chances of children from working-class backgrounds entering higher education and professional occupations changed since the rise of comprehensive education? These are questions we turn to in the next chapter.

5 Educational systems and social mobility

Earlier chapters have mapped a national system of education within which the generative principles of school organisation, pupil allocation and the structures of opportunity seem to have changed considerably. Academic selection at the age of 11 was replaced, for the great majority of children in British state schools, by entry to non-selective secondary comprehensives. In this chapter we explore the extent to which changes in their organising principles have given rise to changes in the life chances of secondary school students, focusing upon social mobility studies.

As a field of study, social mobility research has concerned itself with the interaction between families and social structures. Broadly, it has examined the extent to which family members can, and do, change their social situation and to identify the social features which promote or constrain the possibility of such change. Put more directly, these studies look, for example, at the extent to which children, from working-class families are mobile. This is measured by the volume of children who move in and out of working-class occupations, 'up' the social formation into middle-class jobs and vice versa. These studies are necessarily longitudinal in character, that is, they focus on social change over time. Among their prime concerns are relationships between changes in family opportunities, labour markets, demographic patterns and education. In this chapter we review work that has taken relationships between educational systems and social mobility as its core concern. At first glance, they seem to involve compatible fields of study but both fields appear to have common properties. They are both concerned with intergenerational relations within families and their interaction with social structures. Each field is also concerned to explore the extent to which one generation replicates the social location and status of the previous generation and both fields attempt to understand social processes which promote the reproduction of the social structure, as well as those which interrupt its pattern. There are, however, considerable differences in the intellectual and methodological underpinning of the two fields, despite a considerable overlap in the objects of their studies.

The logics underpinning the work of reproduction theorists lie in their theoretical frameworks which encompass the fields of economic production (the realm of the economy, material production of objects, the circulation of finance) and a field of social production (institutions concerned with the production and circulation of culture, ideas, services). Understanding how production is organised within these fields involves the notion of the division of labour, a socially created arrangement where jobs are apportioned and, in capitalist and other societies, assigned different values and specific locations in a hierarchy of occupations. Social classes have their origins here. Social reproduction theorists have been concerned to examine how institutions and agencies outside the field of economic production, such as families, schools, churches, universities and other cultural institutions, reflect the differentially distributed system of values of the division of labour, asking if and how their social function is to constitute and sustain that division of labour and its associated social classes. The emphasis here is in the degree of what we might call replication. Among the institutions associated with social reproduction, schools have been assigned a key role. It is within their capacity to define and distribute legitimately recognised credentials, modes of thought, cultural and social attributes and networks of association that crucially regulate who goes where within the hierarchy of occupations, positions and careers that define the labour market. We will return to this conceptualisation in Chapter 6. The rest of this chapter, however, has a slightly different focus because social mobility studies see 'replication' as a benchmark to measure the extent to which policy interventions have promoted interruptions within the system. It is to such studies that we now turn to explore how and whether policy frameworks in education have impacted upon inequality.

Social mobility and education

According to a recent, official definition social mobility 'describes the movement or opportunities for movement between different social groups and the advantages and disadvantages that go with this in terms of income, security of employment opportunities for advancement etc.' (Aldridge, 2001: 1). Its mode of analysis features tabulations of the origins and destinations of social groups as measured by their location and entry into a hierarchy of occupational groups. It seeks, for example, to discover the frequency, or likelihood, of sons and daughters achieving occupational statuses which are the 'same as', or 'up', or 'down' from their family of origin. The basic technique of this form of enquiry was what we described earlier as 'political arithmetic'.

Social mobility studies carry policy implications because they are believed to yield insights into the relative 'openess' of social formations, understood to be important because a 'lack of social mobility implies inequality of opportunity' (ibid.). Lack of social mobility can also suggest that patrimony – your family of origin, who you know and your status – determines the life chances of individuals and social groups, rather than credentials, talent or hard work. In these respects social mobility studies are concerned with evidence of the extent to which mobility is present, for whom, the advantages and disadvantages it confers and the effects of policy on social fluidity. For social scientists, such as Goldthorpe (2003) social mobility studies also provide the empirical material to consider changes in social class and evidence to underpin studies of class formation. Of necessity, and in keeping with the purposes of this book, we will limit ourselves to social mobility studies where education is considered directly as a regulator of mobility. We have also selected studies which throw light on the comparative effects of selection and comprehensivisation on educational attainment and, hence, life changes of cohorts of students who experienced particular educational regimes.

Social mobility, selection and comprehensivisation

The transformation of a selective system to a secondary comprehensive system in Britain has become a political battle ground, one based on experiences of and entrenched beliefs in student achievement in one system, as opposed to another. There is almost no middle ground and comparison is almost impossible to do well. The basic research question that numerous studies have sought to answer has been how do students from different social backgrounds fare under contrasting educational systems? The logic of comparing the effectiveness of selective and comprehensive forms would, at first glance, seem relatively straightforward. All 'we need is to observe a set of selective schools and a set of comprehensive schools so as to compare their effects on their students' (Kerckhoff *et al.*, 1996: 233). There are, however, 'inevitable complications' which actually make this very difficult to achieve.

In order to make sure comparisons between the effect of the two systems, it is desirable for students to have experienced only comprehensive or selective education programmes throughout their entire secondary schooling. As Kerckhoff *et al.* argue, the historical development of British secondary education frustrates any attempts at such straightforward comparison. 'Pure' selective and comprehensive systems have not existed side by side. As we have noted, even where LEAs were committed and introduced comprehensive secondaries, there was a tendency to keep 'good' grammars open. In England and Wales by 1970 only ten LEAs had gone fully comprehensive and by 1974 only 42 had done so. In 19 other LEAs no fully comprehensive schools had been established. Where comprehensives existed at all they were usually in LEAs which also contained grammar schools. The problem this gave rise to was that comparable sets of students were unlikely to have attended the two kinds of school. It was unlikely that high ability students would be found in considerable numbers in comprehensives in LEAs where grammar schools existed, obviating the possibility of a rigorous research design based on similar proportions of 'high', 'medium' and 'low' ability students being located in each system, allowing proper comparison to be made of 'system effects'. Given the non-existence of 'pure' systems, Kerkhoff *et al.* concluded that any 'comparison between comprehensive and selective school students is almost certainly going to put comprehensive students at a disadvantage' (p. 234). Therefore, the struggle for researchers was to construct a sample of selective (grammar and secondary modern) and comprehensive schools which were equivalent in their intakes, a criterion difficult to achieve because of the 'creaming' effect of grammar schools on any adjacent comprehensives.

Kerckhoff and his colleagues conducted their comparison using a design that drew on longitudinal data from the National Child Development Study (NCDS) composed of information on 16,000 individuals born in a single week in 1958 and resurveyed when they were aged 7, 11, 16, 23 and 33. They employed data on those students who were at the end of compulsory school in 1974, that is, part of the 1969 secondary entry cohort. Selected students who were in comprehensives established prior to 1970 and were, therefore, likely to have spent their entire secondary schooling in a non-selective system, were matched with students who had spent their entire secondary schooling in grammar and secondary modern schools. Multiple regression analysis systematically compared their academic achievements. Control variables were measures of socio-economic background, gender and scores of general ability measured by tests taken at age 11 as part of the NCDS survey. The dependent variables used were Maths and English test scores at age 16 and secondary school exams passed at age 18. Their findings can be summarised as follows:

1   previous studies that had employed NCDS data tended to show that selective schools enhanced the achievements of those in grammar schools and depressed those of secondary modern students;
2   on two of the three measures, maths test scores and examination scores at age 18+, low ability students had the highest achievement in comprehensive schools. As ability levels increased, however, the comprehensive school advantage decreased, especially on the maths test and in exam performance;
3   within the comprehensive system the mark range was more restricted, with higher ability students doing less well and low ability students doing better than their selective school counterparts; so that
4   in policy terms the authors suggested there were choices about organisation and practice that might be made based either on recognising the depressed range of marks attained by high ability or the enhanced marks of low ability students in comprehensives.

Whichever way we read these results effect sizes are quite low so that difference in effectiveness of one system over another should not be over-interpreted by advocates of either selective or comprehensive education. The authors note that:

> If we accept the estimate of linear change of attending a comprehensive school as ability increases, this means that only 6.9% of the comprehensive school students gained as much as half a point on the 8-point examination measure [while] only 4.2% of students can be said to have gained half a point on examinations by attending a selective (presumably grammar) school.
>
> (Kerckhoff *et al.*, 1996: 248)

With respect of these small differences in 1974, they suggest that grammar schools still enjoyed better staff–student ratios than either secondary moderns or comprehensives and their lower level of teacher attrition provided supportive environments for students. Comprehensives, however, devoted more resources to 'low ability' students with consequent rise in attainments. However:

> Once we controlled for their ability and family background, there was no difference between the average academic achievement of students in comprehensive and selective schools, irrespective of the appropriate samples to be compared.
>
> (Kerekhoff *et al.*, 1996. 252)

There is small comfort for strong advocates of either system when we consider system effects comparatively. In terms of school performance, as conventionally measured by performance in public examinations, who gets what is not greatly influenced by either system. Previous studies, cited by Kerchkoff *et al.*, which they regard as being sound in design and execution, paying proper attention to the socio-cultural composition of student populations at school level, also reported only minor advantages in one direction or the other. Reynolds and Sullivan's (1987) study of nine schools in South Wales compared reading test scores in selective and comprehensive schools located within a socio-economically homogenous area and reported that higher scores were obtained in selective schools. Studies by Gray *et al.* (1983), based on Scottish schools where the social composition of each school was recorded, although no direct measure of ability was available, suggested that there was no dramatic difference in attainment between the two kinds of schools. However, there were slight increases in performance for those attending comprehensive schools, comfort to those alarmed that the demise of selective education would disadvantage categories of pupils formerly educated in grammar schools. Steedman's studies (1980, 1983a, 1983b) employed multivariate analyses of NCDS data to take into account the considerable differences in the socio-economic compositions of comprehensive and selective schools. Again, reporting on maths and reading tests, little or no differences in terms of system effects were reported.

What can we conclude, then, with respect of selective and comprehensive systems, about the intergenerational transmission of educational advantage and disadvantage? On the basis of the empirical evidence which we have so far presented, the answer would have to be, not a great deal. Across the two systems, there remained a close association between individual attributes ascribed by and acquired within families and educational attainment, as measured conventionally by performance in public examinations. Neither system, selective or comprehensive, significantly broke that relationship nor did one reinforce it more than the other. This poses a large question about whether educational policy generally can have any great role in expanding opportunities, decreasing inequalities and promoting social justice. For some answer to these broader questions we turn to studies that have examined longitudinal data on class origins, educational attainment and class destination.

Social mobility, meritocracy and education

In the rest of this chapter we report on studies that have examined empirically the influence of education on the intergenerational transmission of social advantage and disadvantage. In the space available we have to be selective and we have chosen studies primarily concerned with the role of education in relation to trends in social mobility or trends in meritocracy. The studies share common features, such as longitudinal data, political arithmetic approaches to data analysis and the use of 'odds ratios' or similar devices to capture the relative situation of one category of individuals with another. We have also deliberately selected studies which draw on a variety of data sets and employ a variety of analytic techniques. Our view is that if the findings point in broadly the same direction it can be argued that they are secure.

By their nature, these studies all had to overcome, or adjust for, common difficulties, which are noted briefly below. These arise primarily because longitudinal studies capture social systems in change. Common difficulties included:

1   changes in the economy which generated changes in the social division of labour and, thus, the potential for the formation of new social classes which, in turn, shaped the relationship between individual origins and destinations. To give an example, the decline of Britain's manufacturing base, metal-bashing and mining industries generated a decline in the scale and scope of working-class jobs with concomitant reduction in working-class membership. The chances from the 1960s of children from working-class backgrounds ending up in social classes other than that of their origin increased because old occupations were no longer as numerous or available;

2   changes in family arrangements have meant an increase in the number of children brought up in single parent families headed by mothers. As a consequence, this had a negative impact on income levels;

3   changes in levels of poverty and wealth have had consequent effects on the range of educational choices that families can or cannot afford;

4   changes in educational qualifications, such as the ending of O levels and the rise of GCSE, the rise and fall of the Certificate of Secondary Education and the creation of vocational awards, such as National Vocation of Education (NVQ) have all made comparison of 'attainment' over time somewhat difficult;

5   educational polices that have impacted directly on the volume of examination entries, including: permitting secondary modern schools to enter students for O level exams in 1951 and raising the compulsory school leaving age to 16 in 1973, both of which led to rapid expansions of O level entries; and the introduction of course work at GCSE in 1992; and

6   expansion of the higher education sector after the Robbins Report (1966), while more recent policy directions have led to nearly 40 per cent of 18-year-olds entering a greatly expanded range of higher education institutions compared with a tenth of that figure in the immediate postwar period.

While the list is not exhaustive it presents some idea of the factors that have to be addressed in comparative studies that are longitudinal in character.

Social mobility studies focusing on the idea of 'meritocracy' and framing the collection and analysis of empirical data which relate education and the transmission of social advantage and disadvantage have been important. These studies have often taken as a starting point for investigation Daniel Bell's (1960, 1973) hypothesis that post-industrial societies have become more meritocratic insofar as status and income are based on educational credentials and technical competence rather than ascriptive characteristics, such as wealth, social networks and status derived tacitly via the family. The meritocratic framework posits that, over time, the direct relationship between family of origin and the social destination of succeeding generations weakens as the association between educational attainment becomes stronger. This hypothesis has become the starting point for social scientists, such as Halsey (1972), Halsey, Heath and Ridge (1980), Goldthorpe, Llewellyn and Payne (1980), Erikson and Goldthorpe (1992), Marshall *et al.* (1997), Heath (2000) and Goldthorpe (2003) in examining the social role of education in the transmission of social advantage and disadvantage and the extent to which it promotes social mobility. It is these studies which have provided empirical evidence that must be central to any consideration of the relationship between education and social reproduction.

Marshall *et al.* (1997: 74) argued that claims to an increasing meritocracy 'involves claims about changes in the distinct associations between three variables that make up what is sometimes referred to as the 'meritocratic triad'. This can be represented in a variety of forms, as in Diagram A which is to be found in Marshall *et al.* (2004), Goldthorpe (2003) and Prandy (2004). We can perceive change over time by varying the relative strength (+) or weakness of associations (–) between variables. Thus, in non-meritocratic, pre-industrial and industrial societies, class origin and class destination is largely unmediated by education but class destination was strongly determined by class origin (see Diagram 5.2).

Theorists of meritocracy, however, pose the following arrangements which represent a strengthening association between education attainment (see Marshall *et al.*, 1997; Goldthorpe, 2003), as represented in Diagram 5.3. It is this theory that researchers, such as Marshall, Goldthorpe, Prandy aim to test. Has education

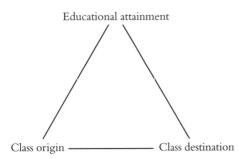

Diagram 5.1 The meritocratic triad (Source: Rogers, 1980: 4)

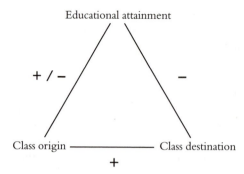

Diagram 5.2 Possible associations between variables

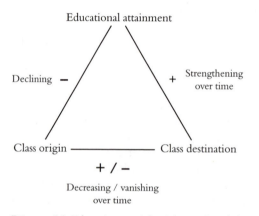

Diagram 5.3 Education, social origins and mobility

assumed a more significant role in the distribution of individuals to places in the class structure or has social class remained the key influence in the structuring of opportunities in and across occupations?

Two key associations have to be tested in order to determine the strength or weakness of the 'meritocratic' argument:

1   To what extent does social class determine educational attainment?
2   To what extent does educational attainment explain the distribution of individuals into occupations?

From these we can infer changes in the direct relationships between class origin and class destination.

We turn first to the exploration by Marshall *et al.* of the associations between education, class origin and class destination. They commence with the view that inferring meritocratic trends from a triad of associations composed of class origin, educational attainment and class destination is fraught with difficulty. They choose instead to examine 'the role of education in mediating the association between origins and destinations and [...] Assess the extent of, and changes over time in, merit-selection by education' (Marshall *et al.*, 1997: 76). In the first phase of their study they pooled information on their sample of over 4,000 individuals who participated in large-scale social surveys in 1986, 1991 and 1992 that included individual's class of origin, class destination (reported via a modified form of the Goldthorpe *et al.* 7-point scale) and educational attainment which, for comparative purposes, had to be re-grouped into 4 levels, level 1 representing low level qualifications and level 4, the highest (degree level or equivalent). They concluded that:

1   there was close association between educational levels achieved and class destination. Those on the lowest level of attainment were least likely to enter the salariat and most likely to enter manual employment with 52 per cent doing so;
2   however, individuals with similar qualifications but different class origins frequently had different class destinations. Individuals from the salariat and other white collar backgrounds were more likely to achieve desirable white collar and salariat occupations. For example, of those in the sample with level 4 qualifications (degrees or equivalent), about 50 per cent of individuals from white collar/salariat backgrounds achieved higher salariat positions, while about 38 per cent of those from unskilled and manual working-class backgrounds did so;
3   in this way 'social origins' 'further to an individual's educational achievements determines his or her class destination' (Marshall *et al.*, 1997: 82);
4   compared with men of similar class origins and educational attainments, women occupied lower rather than higher grade, white collar/salariat positions. This pattern was also repeated in other areas of the labour market where men were more likely than women to obtain skilled rather than unskilled occupations; so that
5   an examination of patterns of education led the authors to conclude that: the reality of modern day Britain is that people from different class origins have unequal chances, not only of educational but also occupational success, despite taking actual credentials into consideration; and these class processes are evident among men and women alike (ibid.: 85).

These findings suggested that there were class-related factors, perhaps socio-cultural features, that work alongside or over and above educational attainment to generate and maintain inter-generational transmission of socio-economic advantage and disadvantage. Quite what these are could not be determined from the data employed in this study.

The second study by Marshall *et al.* looked further at 'trends' in education's mediation of the relationship between class origins and class destinations. In particular, they were concerned to explore whether the connection between social origins and education had changed over the years and impacted on the direct relationship between origins and destinations. In this second phase, pooled data on 11,000 individuals, again gathered from a number of large surveys, was categorised into six groups according to year of birth. The survey captured individuals between ages 18–80 who had been educated in a variety of policy frameworks and indicated that:

1   educational attainment had improved over time, with few people obtaining only the most basic level of education. This applied to both males and females, although differentials in favour of males had been maintained. Females were more likely to achieve only the most basic qualifications and had been less likely to acquire university degrees;

2   educational attainment had improved across all social classes. However, there remained substantial differences between children from working-class and middle-class backgrounds. For example, the proportion of children from unskilled manual working-class backgrounds who achieved only the most basic qualifications fell from 87 per cent (1920s cohort) to 40 per cent (1960s cohort), with concomitant rises in the numbers achieving higher qualifications;

3   working-class children fared much less well at degree level compared to their middle-class counterparts. No more than 9 per cent achieved degrees prior to the 1960s. In that decade the figure rose to 13 per cent. For salariat children, 14 per cent of the oldest cohort achieved a degree, rising to 33 per cent in the 1950s;

4   degree level was probably the most advantageous qualification to have in the labour market and there was a widening gap between social classes. Children from non-manual backgrounds had increasing success, not shared by their counterparts from manual working-class backgrounds, in achieving degree level qualifications. These class inequalities equally affected males and females; and

5   there was a strong association between educational attainment and a person's first category of employment. However, for individuals obtaining similar educational levels of attainment there remained class-related differences about the class of the first employment that they obtained, though the strength of this association declined over the period 1970–90. In that time the odds ratio for men reaching the salariat from class I or class II (salariat/ white collar) backgrounds has halved but became more probable, relative to someone within similar qualifications from unskilled manual backgrounds.

Three broad findings emerged from this study. First, there remained throughout the period covered by the data a strong association between social class and educational attainment for men and women. Second, there was a strong, though uneven, association between educational attainment and destinations in the labour market. For example, 80 per cent of those obtaining degrees or the equivalent ended up in the salariat. Those with the least qualifications were highly likely to end up in working-class occupations. Third, among those with similar or equal qualifications, social class played a part in the eventual allocation of individuals to particular strata within the labour market. Thus, individuals with degrees from white collar/salariat backgrounds were more likely to end up in the most desirable jobs than those from other social class backgrounds. This was again true for both males and females, though women were more likely to occupy positions lower in the occupational hierarchy than males from the same background or with similar qualifications. In other words, social class remained an important sifting and sorting factor in the transmission of intergenerational advantage and disadvantage.

We have taken some time to show the conceptual framework that underpinned, the hurdles that were faced in empirical analysis and the careful nuancing of outputs in this study that uses longitudinal data because they are shared by a number of other social mobility studies. We now turn to some of these other investigations which have prioritised education's role in the transmission of social advantage and disadvantage across generations. We turn first to Goldthorpe, whose work on social mobility and, specifically, how it relates to social class formation has been a central feature of British mobility studies. The paper to which we refer is a brief synthesis of the much larger body of research in which he and his colleagues have been engaged. The paper is short and very accessible but nevertheless demonstrates different techniques for thinking through the triad of origins, education and destination. Again, this paper was concerned to test whether the bond between educational attainment strengthened over time while the direct association between class origin and destination weakened or vanished (Goldthorpe, 2003). Its title, 'The myth of education-based meritocracy: why the theory isn't working' summarises his overall argument that in Britain and across modern societies there is no steady progress towards an educational-based meritocracy. These findings with respect of Britain derived from a study, once again, based on the 1958 NCDS and 1970 British Cohort Study (BCS) surveys. From these data he calculated, via an odds ratio, children's chances, by their mid-twenties, 'of achieving a class position different from their parents, relative to their chances of being found in Class 1' (Goldthorpe, 2003: 236). In other words is 'replication' going on to a greater or lesser degree in other social classes than is found in the salariat? He concluded that:

1   educational attainment was class distributed and the gaps between working and middle-class levels of attainment still persisted, although they had not widened as more working-class children took up available educational opportunities;
2   there were ability differences between children of the higher, salaried class and those of the working class that probably had their origins in 'deep seated' socio-cultural processes (Goldthorpe, 2003: 235). One effect of socio-cultural processes was the influence exerted on children's choice of curriculum subjects, where children from higher, salaried backgrounds are nearly twice as likely to opt for academic courses as their working-class counterparts;

3   education did influence class destination. As Marshall *et al.* (1997) showed, certain qualifications made access to desirable occupations easier. However, according to Goldthorpe, the effects of education on class destination had actually *declined* over the two cohorts from which the data were drawn, in the UK and elsewhere;

4   the importance that employers attached to formal qualifications was less important than previously, especially in relation to higher salaried classes, where socio-cultural resources, acquired tacitly in the family, had become of greater value in the labour market; and

5   overall, children from the least advantaged backgrounds relied more on education to get ahead than their middle-class counterparts who brought other characteristics that employers found desirable to the table. One effect of this was that there was very little downward social mobility in the higher salaried classes.

A contrasting approach has been taken by Prandy and his colleagues (Prandy *et al.*, 2003; Prandy *et al.*, 2004) in the study of intergenerational transmission of social advantage and disadvantage. This study is primarily concerned with the strength of association between fathers' class or origins and sons' and daughters' destinations. Exploring trend data from 1780 to the 1990s, they were able to place mid- and late-twentieth century movements on a much broader historical canvas. The papers referred to are designed as much to explain techniques to specialists in statistical calculations of mobility as to illuminate intergenerational transmission. Our account, therefore, will be brief and an indication of key outcomes only from a complex and carefully nuanced study.

Whereas research by Goldthorpe and others reported generally stable relationships between parents' origins and children's destinations throughout the twentieth century, Prandy *et al.* (2003, 2004) suggested a long-run weakening of this association. The movement toward social mobility has been so gradual that, somewhat amusingly, they calculated that current trends would suggest that it would take another 220–250 years before there were to be no association between fathers' and sons' occupational and social positions. For complicated reasons, 'zero association' between fathers and daughters in this respect would be achieved in half that time (Prandy *et al.*, 2003). Whereas most mobility studies report 'stability' in association between origins and destinations in the twentieth century, they argued that the decline has speeded up rather than remained stable over the most recent cohorts in the study (individuals born 1970–9, 1980–9). One explanation for the 'glacially slow' but nevertheless identifiable change in relationships between origin and destination is education, considered in the 2004 paper, derived from ten large-scale serial surveys supported by the (Economic and Social Research Council (ESRC) and collected between 1963–97 (Prandy *et al.*, 2004). As have others, they record the strong association between class and educational attainment. However, they note a widening in the achievement gap between social classes. The higher the qualifications, the greater the differential, that is, the expansion of higher education has benefited salariat/white collar families more than those of other social classes. Therefore, how does this relate to the central argument advanced previously about weakening the direct bond between fathers' social location and children's destinations? Prandy *et al.* (2004: 8) argued that there had been 'an increased reliance on the educational route as a means of ensuring social reproduction has been accompanied by a decline in the use of alternative resources'. In other words, the route for securing social reproduction, for social and financially advantaged parents at least, has been to ensure a superior education for their children. This did not guarantee entry to the most desirable occupations but gaining the right qualifications was a first step that could be complemented by invoking other socio-cultural resources and social networks. Moreover, as they noted, trends have been both towards a tighter association between class advantage and superior qualifications and a decline in the direct effect of origin on class destination and these have all increased since 1944.

Let us try to summarise Prandy and his associates' conclusions because there are important implications here for the relationship between policy and social reproduction. There are four key points to make:

1 overall, there has been a long-running decline in the extent to which class origin directly influenced class destination. However, this did not mean there was greater 'fluidity' or greater social mobility. Nor could this be straightforwardly interpreted as 'stability' because there was evidence that social advantage continued to be transmitted inter-generationally and, in some respects, gaps between the most and least advantaged classes have widened;

2 education has not served as a mechanism for increasing social mobility, rather it has become the means by which advantages have been transmitted inter-generationally. The process is somewhat complex and varies across classes. Broadly, however, father's occupation has had an increasingly stronger effect on educational attainment so that 'privilege', in one sense, is passed on via a family's capacity to secure superior qualifications for their children. These can then be cashed out via entry to desirable occupations. Where this mechanism ceases to work, socio-cultural and networking resources then play a part in securing entry to desirable occupations. Hence the argument that there has been a decline in the importance of education, for salariat/white collar families, at least;

3 education itself has not become more significant in the determination of class destination. Social origin strongly determines educational attainment, so that education's effects on destination are always influenced by social origins. However, for the least advantaged, education has become more important in the determination of class destination as a resource employed to enter occupations above skilled and non-skilled manual work; and

4 the trends noted above have all increased since 1945. As the Education Act 1944 began to take effect, it brought with it 'a new situation of stability in social reproduction' (Prandy *et al.*, 2004: 19).

We will return to look at the larger implications of this and the previous studies at the conclusion of this chapter. One theme that is very clear is the increasing association between social class and educational attainment. To put further detail into the analysis we turn to one final study which looks at equality and opportunity in education in the UK, with specific reference to the relationship between social class and attainment. It is of added interest because it also comments, *inter alia*, on the relative impact of selective and comprehensive systems of secondary education. Bynner and Joshi (2002) draw on the 1958 and 1970 birth cohort studies described earlier in this chapter to examine whether inequalities and educational outcomes are increasing or decreasing. By drawing on these cohorts they access data on over 11,000 individuals from the 1958 survey and over 8,000 from the 1970 survey educated predominately in two different systems, so that some comparative research is possible. Their descriptive statistics highlight the considerable expansion of numbers of students who have stayed on until aged 16 and who have obtained educational qualifications (see Table 5.1).

The expansion of secondary education and the raising of the school leaving age to 16 in 1973 had effect both in reducing early leaving or drop out figures and greater numbers achieving examination results conventionally recognised by employers and higher education institutions. As Table 5.1 goes on to show, the greatest change was seen in girls and boys who left school without qualifications, where the proportion was halved for boys, and reduced by two-thirds for girls in the 1970 cohort. The table also shows that at the same time there were reductions in the proportion of fathers employed in manual occupations, falling from approximately 70 per cent to about 55 per cent. Levels of poverty remained stable, however, with about 8 per cent in each cohort receiving free school meals. Although the proportion reporting financial hardship fell from 10 to 5 per cent. Class of origin remained a good predictor of early leaving. In the 1958 cohort, for example, sons of unskilled fathers were 16 times more likely to leave than sons of professional fathers. This was halved by 1970. The same pattern, though less extreme, applied to daughters. The higher proportion of parents who had stayed on in the 1970 cohort contributed to the better qualifications obtained by children.

Three sobering findings emerge from this study. First, school examination results are strongly class distributed across both cohorts and pervasively so.

Table 5.1 Changes in examination performance, 1958–70

| | NCDS 1958 | | BCS 1970 | |
	M%	F%	M%	F%
Left school at 16	62	55	49	42
No qualification	14	15	7	5
GCSE grades A–C, NVQ2	30	37	38	43
GCSE 'A' level/NVQ3	18	10	10	12
Degree	14	11	23	19

Source: Bynner and Joshi, 2002: Table 1:0, p. 410.

Controlling for parents' education, Bynner and Joshi claimed that children of skilled manual fathers obtained about one grade less than the children of professional fathers. Second, poverty, as measured by free school meals and other indicators of financial hardship also had negative effects, affecting girls more than boys. Such disadvantages worked primarily through poor primary school performance being carried forward to secondary school, and through family poverty. Third, change from a predominately selective to a comprehensive system has not reduced social inequalities in education for girls or boys.

How does such a school focused study relate to larger patterns of intergenerational mobility? It fits in well with further evidence, if any more is needed, from studies conducted by researchers at the Centre for Economic Performance (CEP) at the London School of Economics (LSE), an important player in public policy debates and identified with strong argument *against* increased social mobility and *for* the greater capacity of middle and professional classes to pass on advantages to their children. They have showed that the gap between professional middle class and working-class educational performance noted above corresponded with the broader patterns of inter generational transmission. Taking into account income data collected in 2000, they argued that children from more privileged backgrounds were likely to enter the labour market and earn more than those from less privileged families, even when educational qualifications were similar. This 'flatly contradicts the common view that anyone can make it in modern Britain. Indeed, rather than weakening, the link between an individual's earnings and those of his or her parents has strengthened' (Blanden *et al.*, 2002: 3). This study and that of Galindo-Rueda and Vignoles (2003) drew, yet again, on the two birth cohort studies mentioned above for their primary data and added income data collected in 2000 for the second (1970) cohort.

What findings support the contention of Blanden *et al.* that 'not everyone can make it' in modern Britain? Their technique is to compare the relationship between income and education of the family of origin with income levels achieved by children in 1958 and 1970. An intermediary device, the immobility index, measured for the two cohorts the extent to which social mobility had or had not occurred. In more simple language they ask whether there is evidence that income levels of wealthy families have been maintained by their children or experienced a downward shift and, in comparison, what proportion of children from low income families have moved up into higher income brackets than their parents. Social mobility would be evidenced by downward movement intergenerationally from high incomes to lower incomes and clear movement from lower incomes to higher incomes, in roughly the same proportions. In summary, Blanden *et al.* found that:

1   in the 1958 cohort, sons from families that earned two times more than other families, earned approximately 12 per cent more than their less well endowed counterparts by the time they reached their early thirties. For the 1970 cohort, however, the figure has increased to 30 per cent, so tightness of the association between family of origin and children's incomes, for higher income families, substantially increased, both for sons and daughters;

2   the fall in social mobility has arisen, in part, from the expansion of higher education, which had benefited children of higher income families most. Able children from poor families have been able to realise new opportunities to attend HE institutions and this, in turn, has meant an unequal distribution of HE qualifications and higher incomes. For example, in the 1990s participation rates for lower middle and working class families (social classes D and E) rose from 11 to 16 per cent of the age cohort while, for middle and professional classes (A–C), it rose from 26 to 36 per cent, about double the percentage increase;

3   whereas in the 1958 cohort the sons of the richest parents by the age of 30 would earn 113 per cent more than the sons of the poorest parents. In the 1970 cohort they earned 138 per cent more; and

4   when the immobility index for education and income was applied across the two cohorts, in almost all cases a higher proportion of children remained in the same quartile as their parents in the 1970 cohort than was the case in the 1958 sample. Thus, for example, while in the 1958 NCDS cohort, 17 per cent of sons and 18 per cent of daughters whose origins are in the bottom quartile for income rose to the top, in the 1970 BCS cohort only 14 per cent of sons and 15 per cent of daughters did so. At the other end of the scale, 19 per cent of sons and 18 per cent of daughters fell to the bottom of the scale in the NCDS cohort, while in the 1970 cohort the figures were 14 and 13 per cent, respectively. This reduction in upward and downward movement through the quartiles represented a pattern of reduced mobility.

Much of these widening gaps in income stemmed from greater use by richer families of the opportunities afforded by expansion of higher education.

A somewhat different approach to the question of the relationship between education and social mobility has been taken by two other CPE researchers, Galinda-Rueda and Vignoles (2003). We do not discuss their work in any great detail, but touch on it because it confirms the trends reported by Blanden *et al.* They begin with the assumption that in a meritocratic society there would be a close association between cognitive ability, educational performance and labour market access. In other words, the most able would achieve the best exam performances and higher paid, more prestigious occupations. For them, a counter indicator would be evidence that educational performance and labour market access remained class distributed so that, in fact, exam performance and occupations were closely associated with family of origin. So they asked whether the most able did best in school exams and social class determined education performance and labour market access. And did education promote or act as a barrier to social mobility? Their evidence is drawn, as with Blanden *et al.*, from the 1958 and 1970 birth cohort studies whose participants, it will be recalled, sat benchmark tests, providing a source of comparison about cognitive ability and social class. They boldly claim that:

The effect of cognitive ability on educational attainment has actually decreased, while the role of parental social class and income in determining educational attainment has increased. In other words the British education system has become less meritocratic.

(Galindo-Rueda and Vignoles, 2003: np)

The paper statistically modelled the highest achieved academic qualification (GCSE, A level, degree etc.) as the dependent variable, against ability and family characteristics (income, occupation, involvement in child's education). They argued that the models they produced relate a family's propensity to invest in education to qualification and labour market access. One question that arises from this line of investigation is the extent to which ability or income determines an individual's propensity to obtain more education. They concluded that, for the 1958 cohort, 'the effect of ability was almost independent of income. For the 1970 cohort the positive effect of ability is only noticeable for those with higher family income' (Galindo-Rueda and Vignoles, 2003: 112–13). Therefore, for the later cohort, for children of higher income families only, cognitive ability led to chances of higher qualifications and incomes. This did not apply to high ability children in lower income families. In more detail, patterns of interaction of social class, family income and cognitive ability suggest that, for girls in the highest quartile of ability but in the bottom income quartile, chances of obtaining a degree went down from 30 per cent to 28 per cent between the cohorts while, for girls whose families were in the top income quartile, the probability increased from 60 per cent to 70 per cent. Much the same held true if social class was employed as a variable alongside ability. For sons of professionals in the top ability quartile, chances of entering university increased from 76 per cent to 85 per cent, while the chances for unskilled workers reduced from 40 per cent to 19 per cent. Ability alone did not explain who made it to the top or not. Less able children from higher income families and professional backgrounds were more likely to participate in higher education than their working-class counterparts, whether they were boys or girls. On this basis the authors suggest that the British system was still class ridden, with scant evidence of social mobility.

Conclusion

We stated at the outset that we would, of necessity, be selective in the studies which we reported. Each of those considered in this chapter is concerned with the inter-generational transmission of socio-economic advantage and dis-advantage. They address how fluid society is and how much movement can be observed between social classes. Social reproduction in terms of the extent to which social advantage and disadvantage is passed across generations has been explored specifically by Prandy *et al.*, Goldthorpe and others. Persistent patterns are reported in these studies, although differences occur in aspects of their interpretation and in explanation of processes of intergenerational transmission. Whatever else these studies show they confirm that the links between social class, opportunity and attainment, first noted in the studies on grammar school entry prior to 1944, are as pervasive today. While expansion of secondary and higher education provision has benefited families of all social classes, children from the salariat/white collar classes have done so most and a 'gap' has been maintained between them and children from working-class families. While the upper reaches of the occupational structure have been opened to anyone achieving appropriate educational qualifications, entry to them is achieved disproportionately by children of families already socially located at this level. Moreover, there is little evidence of their downward mobility. Socio-cultural forces, unspecified in these studies, are invoked to explain why middle-class families successfully achieve intergenerational transmission of social advantages

What, then, are the implications for educational policy, social inequalities and social reproduction? The expansion of secondary education after 1944, establishment of a tripartite system and its subsequent replacement by one predominately comprehensive in character, expansion of higher education, cessation of the traditional apprenticeship and the development of vocational routes in secondary and further education have not greatly redistributed class chances in education, nor have they substantially reduced inequalities. Neither targeted nor universal policy initiatives have blunted the close associations between social origin, educational attainment and subsequent employment prospects in a changing labour market, though there are marginal gender differences in the size of effects on opportunity and attainment. The question remains as what would need to be done to achieve such ends.

6 Bernstein, social reproduction and intergenerational transmission

Introduction

For social mobility theorists, intergenerational transmission involves a three-sided relationship between the family, education and occupation. While the cumulative direction of social mobility studies leaves us with some puzzles about the relationship between educational policy, changes in the education system and patterns of equality and attainment, research has shown that education increasingly mediates the direct relationship between the family (origin) and occupation (destination). More precisely, the specific education and credentials that are acquired crucially regulate who gets what in the labour market. Yet puzzles remain. Why, for example, has the shift from selection to comprehensivisation had so little effect on 'gaps' in attainment and why have middle and professional-class children not only retained but seemingly increased their capacity to capture jobs in desirable sectors of the labour markets? Does this represent a 'failure' of policy or simply its incapacity to transform aspects of the social structure that enable the transmission of inequalities to persist regardless of policy attempts to interrupt social reproduction? These are questions that social mobility theorists cannot really answer without sociologically rich accounts and insights into structure and processes in the two sites which regulate inter-generational transmission of opportunity and equality, the family and school. Whereas the relations and conditions of production ultimately determine the possibilities for 'reproduction', the family and school are the sites where social, linguistic, cognitive, cultural and educational identities are created and transmitted. For a greater understanding of the role of the family, the school and their interrelationships with respect of intergenerational transmission we turn to Bernstein's work.

In discussion of inter-generational transmission of equality and inequality, Bernstein employed an analytic framework composed of the family, the school, and the division of labour, not unlike the triad of social mobility theorists. There were significant differences between them, however, not least in his emphasis on mothers in the process of intergenerational transmission. His focus clearly emphasised the positional, interpersonal and communicative properties of relationships within families and schools. The character of the linkage between language and control was paramount. His language of description, drawn from a very wide range of social theorists, linguists, psychologists and sociologists set his work apart not only from the much narrower field of social mobility but most other educational theorists and researchers. From Bernstein's early work, it was possible to derive two kinds of explanation for the relatively unchanging character of the patterns of intergenerational transmission of inequality and the low capacity for educational policy to interrupt it. The first related to inter-relationships between the relevant elements of the social structure, the family, school and division of labour. The second related more specifically to the field of education and the social function of what he calls 'pedagogic discourse' which he continued to elaborate over a period of thirty years. We will deal with each explanation in turn.

Pedagogic discourse: family, school and work

Throughout his developing theory and research, while the emphasis laid upon and the delineation and character of one of more of its elements shifted from time to time, Bernstein always held the triad of family, school and work at the centre of his theory of social reproduction. What was important in Bernstein's work and is directly relevant to our task here is that each are sites of social reproduction and each generate the possibilities of what can be transmitted, what can be acquired and by whom. While much of his work examined categories, processes and identity work conducted in each of these sites, what was important were their inter-relationships. Education policy, therefore, may be grounded in notions of, and seek to achieve, equality of opportunity and this may be the overt intention of schools and teachers but it cannot eliminate the generation, maintenance or transmission of inequalities either in the work place, family or even the school curriculum.

Let us take the argument one stage further by looking at one part of the 'triad', work, or as Bernstein sometimes referred to it, the field of production. This is the source of the division of labour, the kinds of occupation and occupational structure – the 'destiny' – into which families and schools distribute children/students. It is hierarchical in structure and, thus, it transmits inequalities in power, status and income. The division of labour also changes in character, projecting different possible 'futures' or 'destinies' inter-generationally. By generating the occupational categories, the relations between them, the places and spaces that are available as 'futures' and 'destinies', the field of production, in effect, generates 'what' is to be reproduced. We have already noted that decline in the UK industrial base has meant a reduction in stable employment with steady wages for school leavers with few or no qualifications.

An equally pertinent example can be taken from the other end of the division of labour that relates directly to the middle classes' capacity to reproduce their social location and standing. Recent work by Brown and his colleagues has specifically focused on the graduate labour market what employers seek in graduate trainees and the processes by which companies and corporations select them from the graduate 'pool' (Brown and Hesketh, 2004; Smetherham, 2004). One key finding is the extent to which employers now place value on 'soft skills' alongside, of course, conventional degree qualifications. 'Soft skills' in this context mean good communication, ease of rapport with others and capacities for mediation and negotiation. Employers value these because graduates represent 'the face' of the company in the wider world, they 'fit in', promising creative continuity.

From a Bernsteinian perspective these are qualities strongly associated with and tacitly acquired through the 'invisible pedagogy' that characterised the family interactions of the 'new' middle classes. These classes were grounded in the field of reproduction and their position was maintained and reproduced via their capacity to manipulate and be at ease with cultural and symbolic goods. In the labour market achieving a degree signalled acquisition of specialised knowledge and technical mastery, getting graduates to the starting gate but, increasingly, it was the distribution of soft skills that operated as an additional factor in deciding how fast and in what precise career direction they went. Inequalities in how positions are distributed and prepared for continue to be generated, regardless of policy changes, in the field of education. Families and education, however tacitly, are engaged in the distribution of children/students to this occupational structure.

Education policy cannot fundamentally change the social functions of education in a situation where the division of labour determines the volume and range of possible 'destinies' for those in school. Neither can it determine what attributes are to be valued in the labour market, nor which are convertible into particular careers or not. This means that there are properties within the field of education that articulate and reflect those in the other sites of social reproduction, the family and work. Changes in education policy struggle to affect how these become embedded in the field of education. In his very last published text, for example, Bernstein (2001a) referred to the new curricular emphasis on 'train-ability', 'a regionalised, market-based, performance pedagogy' as being 'socially empty' because, as we saw in Chapter 1, it fails to recognise that responding to a future presupposes a prior, specialised identity. When 'training' becomes all, simply seen as a technology; by 'submerging regulative discourse [...] pedagogy loses any sense of a moral trajectory, of any grounding in a social base' (Muller, 2004: 4). The apparently disinterested appeal to 'necessity' or the 'public interest' in educational policy may often mask complicity with the needs of capital or vested interest, on the one hand, and naiveté about the limits of the possible, on the other.

Pedagogic discourse: policy and reproduction

How is it within the field of education that over a sixty-year period, covering myriad policy initiatives and adaptations, administrative guidelines and codes of practice, the gap between middle-class and working class students' attainment has changed so little? How has the field remained the site for the reproduction of these differences in light of such attempts to change it? What is it in the field that has remained seemingly immutable? Here again, we turn to Bernstein's language of description to provide an explanation of the seeming incapacity of education to reform patterns of educational inequality.

For Bernstein, education was a field with 'specialised interests' with a discourse that distinguished it from other fields. It was specialised by virtue of its institutions (schools, colleges, universities), agents (education ministry officials, LEA officers, teachers) and focus on the education and training via formal schooling, further education and university participation of students. As with other fields, it was an arena of struggle between interests competing to define its rules (or 'device') as to what was to be counted as legitimate knowledge, identity and practice. Their outcomes mattered because it was only legitimate knowledge that was credentialed via public examination results, vocational qualifications or degrees. Moreover, this knowledge was made available in highly regulated terms of transmission and receipt. It was more easily recognised and worked with by some people rather than others.

In any field, how legitimate knowledge, including policy texts, are assembled and transmitted is a systematic activity whose rules are expressions of society's wider distribution of power and control. Initial assembly of policy texts tends to take place within the education field at the 'official pedagogic contextualisation' level, which is broadly equivalent to the state, its departments and agents. Texts or dominant frameworks of meaning are successively and selectively appropriated by subordinated fields, the pedagogic recontextualising field and the field of reproduction. Ball and his associates (e.g. Bowe *et al.*, 1992) referred to much the same character of policy process in their 'contexts' of 'influence', 'text production' and 'practice', while politicians and globalisation theorists tell us that these contexts have an increasingly international flavour. This basic structure remains unchanged, although occupants of these fields or levels may alter and the contents of the texts that are assembled and reproduced change pedagogic discourse, the means by which dominant frameworks of meaning, embedded in legitimate knowledge or authoritative texts, are made available, tends to be a top down activity wherever it occurs, whether in families, workplaces, media or leisure contexts. Nowhere has this been more so than in education where the divide between those who know and those who are to be initiated has been its key organising principle. So what dominant frameworks or texts have dominated the field of education and how have these remained stable?

We already have plenty of detail to put into this somewhat abstract system. It can be argued that the pedagogic discourse that has dominated the last 60 years of British secondary education was assembled from the late 1930s and consolidated in the 1944 Education Act and its aftermath. At that time the 'educational state' might have been said to 'know its place' and the official agencies with which it surrounded itself were sparse and 'influence' was regularly invited though the variously constituted Central Advisory Committee memberships of the great and the good who 'reported' on specific issues remitted to them. While the state had actively intervened in the curriculum and methods of elementary schools since 'payment by results' in the 1870s, it was the prospect of a possibly strengthened Labour government that persuaded Sir Eustace Percy and the

Conservatives (with Liberal and, more oddly, Labour compliance), to withdraw from doing so, as we observed in Chapter 1 (White, 1975). Secondary schools, long in the thrall of the Board's regulations until 1945 were thereafter left simply to the examination boards and the universities that largely controlled them. In a period of postwar 'partnership' between central and local government and the churches, teachers, though associationally divided, were regularly consulted, legislative activity was low and LEAs ruled their territories. In some places LEAs ruled with a rather baronial authority, and in others with great diffidence. What we referred to as the grassroots rise of the comprehensive helps explain that, while it may have been a 'movement' with an ensemble of pedagogic recontextualising agents, among which we might regard organisations like CASE and the Schools' Council, the latter devoted to the development of curricular and pedagogic forms for the new order, it never became a 'system'. Selective education remained undisturbed in some LEAs and constituted high status competition in many others so that the regulative principles of the system never transcended those of its selective past. The new secondary school forms emulated rather than innovated.

Whereas much of the primary school system, particularly as the 11+ died, moved toward more child-centred pedagogic modalities, from performance to competence, comprehensives struggled, largely unsuccessfully, to modify grammar school practices. This was partly an issue of hoping to inherit their standing, but also of failure to successfully elucidate new pedagogic rules that engaged parents and students in 'different' school and classroom patterns. Even in the wake of the Newsom Report (Central Advisory Council for Education (CACE), 1963) that delineated the underperformance of ordinary and less able pupils, school practices and forms that offered more than cosmetic challenge, from in-service 'Newsom Courses' (e.g. James, 1968), to events such as those at Risinghill School (Berg, 1968), or the much maligned Schools' Council Humanities Project, tended to receive short shift, fuelled by media opprobrium. By the 1970s, the ubiquity of comprehensives had, in some areas, created problems even for aspiring working and middle-class families who had often initially welcomed them, not least because they offered to end some of the iniquities of 11+. These were variously expressed as inadequacies of curriculum, grouping, ethos or order and the character of their staff and/or student bodies. Governments, who had reluctantly moved in their favour now, following Callahan's damascene moment in Ruskin College in 1976 and Thatcher's ascension to the elected monarchy in 1979, quickened in disbelief. The latter's earliest moves were symptomatic, ejecting teachers from consultation and collective bargaining and ending industry-wide labour training schemes (Esland, 1996; Davies and Evans, 2001).

A 'strong state' now awakened, determined to put education in its place, with a much increased legislative tempo and a rapidly multiplying retinue of official recontextualising agents. Having played earlier with moving key educational policy making and administration out of a moribund DES into departments with more straightforwardly economic and labour force responsibilities, policy under Thatcher settled for emasculating the LEAs, who were not necessarily obedient, reforming HMI which, while conveniently being 'independent', generally was obedient, and extending their activity to control and regulate a school system that was given managerial and budgetary 'freedom'. But such considerations bring us firmly into the concerns of the next two chapters and will be dealt with more fully there. Meanwhile, we note once more here that Bernstein (1990) repeatedly claimed that pedagogy had no voice of its own, that it simply relayed those of others. Its 'relations to' class, gender and ethnicity were 'seen as the main engines of educational and social change', to which we would add policy change (or not), rather than articulation of its 'relations within' (Tyler, 2004: 16). Nothing changes in that respect. Impelled by a rhetoric of economic nesessity, as Tyler points out, recent policies on 'lifelong learning, trainability and ready and pervasive access to information technology', celebrating 'endless forming and reforming of individual desire' (Tyler, 2004: 18) are producing a world, dominated by markets and consumerism, that Bernstein (2001a, 2001b), somewhat ironically, depicted as our newly emerging Totally Pedagogised Society (TPS). Here, managed by a reforming 'strong state', 'a new cadre of pedagogues, with their research projects, recommendations, new discourses and legitimations are being constructed' (loc. cit.: 367) and new, largely undiscussed, pedagogic processes that point to prospective rather than retrospective identities assume heightened importance. In Muller's (2004: 5) view this, once more, is to ignore Bernstein's advice to 'educators to turn their gaze away from ideological critique of the external lineaments of pedagogy to the conditions for its effectiveness'.

Pedagogic discourse: its key features

In our account of the creation of the postwar secondary education system, outlined in Chapter 2, it was argued that, drawing on empirically weak but culturally deeply embedded categories, it was widely held that children could be regarded as having one of three kinds of ability and aptitude. Moreover, with socio-metric test scores supplementing measures of school attainment, it was asserted that students could be placed accurately in educationally appropriate categories. Such sifting and sorting mechanisms as we have described here have been employed, in somewhat different ways, as central features of British secondary education for the last 60 years. They chiefly explain why schools remain our prime, official site for social reproduction. The mechanism is not only, in Bernstein's terms, a 'message system' about who and what are regarded as superior and inferior within it but bestows curricular and pedagogic advantages selectively on those categorised as able rather than less able. Children of professional and middle-class families have been disproportionately its beneficiaries. The question is, then, how has this system remained in place for so long? Answers to this take us to the heart of the social functions of education.

Sifting and sorting

First, sifting and sorting mechanisms – from the 11+, banding, setting and streaming policies, the allocation of students to vocationally or academically orientated courses, to special educational needs programmes – are expressions of larger structures of power and control that are external to education. The hierarchy of occupations within the division of labour and the historic scarcity of places in British higher education has pressured schools to identify and give children credential with different types and levels of qualifications. Employers and universities have made it clear that this is the key function of schools. For example, GCSE's are graded A★–G, all of which signal a 'qualification', yet employers, universities and, more recently, governments have made it abundantly clear that only grades A★–C constitute a 'pass' at this level. Other grades have little or no credence in the job market.

Second, there has been sustained ideological combat, led by commentators purportedly concerned with 'standards', for qualifications that unambiguously identify the 'best and brightest' and mark them via an experience in a strongly classified, subject-dominated, secondary curriculum and by unique credentials (see Benn and Chitty, 1996). For this reason we have had sustained struggles, thus far successful, to retain grammar schools, extend church, subject specialist and, in Wales, Welsh medium schools (all proxies for some measure of selection). The addition of a 'starred' grade A award at A level is imminent, strongly supported by the fee-paying sector primarily in a bid to sustain its claim to excellence and, thus, further mark it off from the state sector and by elite universities. On the other hand, others have argued (O'Keefe and Stoll, 1995) that, *inter alia*, 'traditional' subjects, compulsorily imposed on all 14–16-year-olds, cause truancy (now at a recent high in our secondary schools) because some categories of students, by no means always low-achieving, either see schools as reneging on their promise of 'quality' classroom experience or little or no relevance in the formal study of, say, foreign languages. Proposed new pathways for 14–16-year-olds (DfES, 2003) may well consecrate both the 'hard' and 'soft' categorisation of students and project them, at an early date and to different career paths as part of our TPS.

Third, such categorisation of students has directly benefited middle-class families, privileging their children with better qualified teachers, providing curriculum pathways to longer school careers, in a system where school resources increase with the age of students. Different fractions of the middle class, however, have secured educational privilege by different means. The old middle class, whose standing largely derived from the ownership or control of the making and selling of 'things', have tended to be the traditional users of the fee-paying public and direct grant grammars. The new middle class, now artlessly referred to as joint controllers of the 'means of enunciation' (Davies, 1994: 19) have benefited from the retention of grammar schools, catchment area school admission policies which enabled them to secure places in desirable state schools through the purchase of appropriate housing at premium rates, greater under-standing and manipulation of rules of entry to quasi-selective schools and allocation of their children to upper sets in comprehensive schools. Here there has been the sustained and justifiable belief that schools should recognise that students had a range of aptitudes and talents and that curriculum and pedagogy, ideally, should be matched to student competencies. While compelling, the argument is one which can, and has been, also employed to justify setting, streaming, banding and 'tiered papers'. We have seen that the great majority of comprehensive schools have always adopted some form of homogeneous ability-based pupil grouping beyond their early years. The publication of school performance tables based on Key Stage test and public examination results and the introduction of tiered papers have pushed such practices not only back into the lower age groups in secondary schools but into primary schools where streaming was, of course, until thirty years ago, a perfectly ordinary sight (Barker-Lunn and Ferri, 1970; Jackson, 1970). Gillborn and Youdell's (1999) study of how secondary schools select and support students on the borderline of C grade so as to maximise their chances of obtaining grades A*–C used officially to decide school excellence showed how sifting and sorting has become not only an embedded element but a detailed, individualised technology in secondary school practice. All of these cases constitute original, grassroots, recontextualisations of pedagogic discourse which had its origins at the official level and whose initial intention may or may not have been to engender them. There is very considerable evidence to show that, at the level of the classroom, teachers' predominantly ability group homogeneously for teaching purposes, even when the school's organising principle in its allocation students to classes celebrates heterogeneity, or mixture, even in primary schools.

There are numerous indications as to how the discourse has been selectively taken up by institutions in the pedagogic recontextualising field. LEAs, for example, once very much mediators of official policy, now so shrunken that they may be better thought of as among its reproducers, from the late 1940s adopted, not without concern in some cases, sifting and sorting via age 11+ admission policies. As comprehensives appeared, they instituted rather than resisted social and academic selection through catchment area policies (see Chapter 4). Examination boards, albeit largely at the behest of schools and educationalists, introduced course work as a major element in age 16+ examinations, in effect increasing the already huge subsidy noted by Bernstein as available to students whose families were in positions to help, directly or in resource terms, with school work. It also tended to favour the learning and work styles of girls rather than boys, accelerating their 'catching up', then exceeding of the latter's examination achievements. Private agencies and individuals offering 'coaching' for examinations, while achieving nowhere near the scale of operations achieved in some of our 'succeeding' Pacific-rim competitors, such as Taiwan, Japan and South Korea, have become a further, as yet unresearched, area of overwhelmingly class subsidy. The ability of schools themselves to offer extra, individual or small group tutorial is increasing but limited, often targeted, as we have just noted above, to shifting those at the margin of the A*–C band. Mentoring schemes involving university students taking secondary pupils under their wing are growing. Anecdotal evidence suggests that as much as 40 per cent of secondary students now receive some sort of private coaching, particularly in maths and the sciences. Publishers are increasingly engaged not only in the creation of textbooks but of study guides and revision notes. Target setting and benchmarking of attainment within school improvement plans, arising out of uncritical official adoption of private sector practices, in pursuit of the bonuses in achievement guaranteed to those following the managerialist algorithms derived from school effectiveness research, have also tended to promote sorting by ability. Indeed, all these social forces, we suggest, have sustained sifting and sorting at the centre of official pedagogic discourse and many contemporary trends in educational policy decisions are expanding its possibilities. The operation of policies of 'diversity and choice', such as those which enabled grammar schools in the 1990s to seek the shelter of grant-maintained status to keep off LEAs which sought to reorganise them along comprehensive lines receive special attention in Chapter 8.

In Bernstein's terms, the boundaries between categories, whether curriculum subjects, or ability groups, are expressions of power. How and why particular students are allocated to particular categories is an aspect of control, exercised in most cases by schools. The system has remarkable capacity for absorption, what curriculum researchers in the 1970s, reflecting on schools' capacities for Schools' Council projects to sink within them without trace, following their adoption, referred to as 'innovation without change'. Among the most outstanding example of this during our period was the fate of the Conservative 'industrial trainers' inspired Manpower Services Commission who funded the Technical and Vocational Education Initiative (TVEI) which, from the mid-1980s to the mid-1990s, set out to create local work-related courses in schools and colleges. Fund recipients were required to sign contracts 'which promised a countervailing of gender and ability biases in providing extended vocational options in years 4 and 5 (now referred to as 9 and 10) of secondary school, with activity and pupil-negotiative emphasis' but whose 'category-disturbing impact [...] was largely confined to raising the canniness of teachers about outside change agents' (Gleeson, 1989), 'new vocationalism' largely reaching pupils of the middle ability range, in well-resourced contexts 'by teachers who welcomed the borrowing of practices from further education which permit them to treat pupils more like clients' (Davies, 1994: 24–5). The City Technology Colleges that followed them have proved, as we will see in Chapter 8, to be something of a political embarrassment.

The replacement of timed examinations by course work in the 1990s has been a further, important example of how a complete change, in this case in cherished assessment practice was absorbed into the everyday framework of activity and meaning in schools and classrooms. We believe that this normalising capacity, rooted in both the interests and practices of producers and clients, relying on deeply held beliefs in how subjects and children are and teaching and learning should be, is the source of their durability and conditions the capacity of policy to transform systems. Taking its meaning in the broad sense of 'how the work is done', we have long known that schools and classrooms are low technology operations and, where technology is weak, values serve as substitutes (Davies, 1973, 1976, 1994). This is likely to remain the case until we begin to grasp the implications of work, such as that by Ana Morais and her associates that carefully anatomises the embeddedness of instructional in regulative discourse and how careful manipulation of its component parts may alter capacities to achieve and, in particular, allow lower working-class achievement levels to be brought up to those of their better endowed peers.

Privileging practices

The answer embedded in Bernstein's early work represented in the papers collected in *Class, Codes and Control, Volume 1* (Bernstein, 1971) as to how education ensured reproduction was that schools selectively identified, privileged and rewarded certain kinds of language use, orientations to knowledge and behavioural attributes. In one sense this was their acknowledged social function. They were required to orientate students towards particular knowledge domains, embed specific modes of thinking, make legitimate specialised modes of pedagogy and attempt to ensure that students acquired capacities to enter and sustain particular forms of social relationships with teachers and their peers. This 'constellation of orientations' (Atkinson, 1985: 52) that were constitutive of schools were regarded by educationalists in the 1970s (and in some unreconstructed consciousnesses even still) as largely identified with language use. But the fuller implications of Bernstein's insistence that language use was inseparable from orientation towards knowledge and social relationships, of which different sorts were tacitly acquired within middle and working-class families, went very largely unheeded. 'The school', he noted, 'is an institution where every item in the present is finally linked to a distant future, consequently there is no clash of expectations between the school and the middle class child'. Furthermore, he argued 'there is little conflict of values between teachers and the middle-class child and, more importantly, the child is predisposed to accept and respond to the language structure of communication' (Bernstein, 1971: 29). Middle-class children inherited, via family interaction and communication, what he initially called 'formal' language use (later renamed elaborated code) (Bernstein, 1971: 28). Among other things, it permitted comparison and contrast between objects and links between them and 'distant futures'. Its possession enabled tacit ways of orienting to objects, texts and interactive relationships that were cognate with schools' orientation to knowledge and social relations. Students without the facility to evoke and employ elaborate code were unable to realise the potential that school offered and, indeed, might 'resist' its instrumental and expressive cultures. For this minority of working-class children and their families the mutuality with school that we noted above was reversed. Schools operated and privileged an ensemble of orientations, dominated by particular control relations associated with and acquired through elaborated code use that some working-class students found difficult to access and, in some cases, resisted in ways that were translated by schools into imputations of low ability and poor or inappropriate behaviour.

While Bernstein imputed no 'lack' or 'deficit' to working-class speech or culture his ideas, based on long-term and detailed fieldwork (see, particularly Bernstein, 1973), were doubly misunderstood. Perhaps most importantly, his message was garbled in its transmission to teachers, mainly during their initial training, as meaning that working-class children, in virtue of the character of their language, were incapable of school success. This was particularly hurtful to someone whose instincts were deeply egalitarian and who argued that, if there was a fault or problem, then it lay with the schools, whose obligation it was to take on children 'where they were'. Indeed, perhaps his best known, but least understood dictum, was that 'education cannot compensate for society' (Bernstein, 1970: 344). No child or family lacked 'culture', rather pedagogic discourse was founded on different linguistic, cognitive and control principles from those transmitted within working-class families. While as a matter of fact and source of sorrow the social function of schools was not to facilitate the reproduction of social and cultural qualities that characterised working-class life, their obligation was to accept them as datum and to seek to provide the means for all children to access decontextualised, as well as local, meanings requiring facility in both restricted and elaborated codes.

There were also academic attacks, most hurtfully from Labov (1972) in the USA who claimed that Bernstein saw middle-class language as superior in all respects and denied the existence, let alone the measurability, of such codes and their purchase on black, urban speech. In Britain, Rosen (1974) rightly charged Bernstein 'with overgeneral use of class terms, which he would like to see corrected not by continual precise reference to the samples used in the reported research but with a substitute Marxist vocabulary' (Davies, 1976: 172) that would reveal the dominant culture overvalued and the dominated one undervalued. Along with the undoubtedly overgeneralised use of the class terms, perhaps most damaging to the version of this vital debate as it entered educational discourse was that the failure to understand, both by academics and teachers that it was not about *linguistics* but *sociolinguistics*, less about particularities of syntax and grammar than about family and school communication and *control* relationships.

Bernstein was very clear that he found his position to be uncomfortable. On the one hand he held the view that, unless lower working-class children's 'forms of consciousness, their way of being in the world [...] is active in the school [...] there can be little change in the children or in the society'. On the other, he saw 'that the code which facilitates the *systematic* examination of, and change in, the boundaries of experience is not initially made available to the children as an essential part of their socialisation within the family' (Bernstein, 1975: 28). Children who did not share the same world of cognitive orientations, praise and blame as their teachers, whose categorical world was specific rather than general and whose control orientation might be to shame rather than guilt were condemned never to meet as minds with those teachers who not only had no inkling of this divide but, indeed, used it as a source of invidious comparison in pupil labelling. The thread that runs right through from Bernstein's earliest work on family communication structures to his work on formal schooling is that instructional discourse depends upon or is embedded in regulative discourse. Understanding their empirical combination in detail is work still largely to be done and, when pursued with detailed care, is capable of surprise. Hasan, one of Bernstein's earliest collaborators in his sociolinguistic research has noted, for example, how in her recent research in Sydney kindergarten classes the semantic (content) 'orientation of classroom talk was an exaggerated version of middle-class mothers' semantic orientation while its framing (control) was an exaggerated version of working-class mothers; single minded devotion to one context' (Hasan, 2001: 72). Manipulating either version so as to draw children more effectively into learning presupposes that teachers have anatomised them and have the will and means to manipulate them appropriately (Neves *et al.*, 2004).

But these considerations are not part of the current terms of debate let alone that of the 1960s and 1970s that did little or nothing to alter the constitutive principles of either primary or secondary education as it moved, unevenly, from selective to comprehensive. In Bernstein's terms, these changes in organisational form left the character of dominant pedagogic discourse virtually untouched. Schools' capacity to privilege the bearers of elaborated codes and associated modes of thought and orientation to control, whatever their social origins, provide some of the explanation for the durability of the gap between middle-class and working-class educational attainment.

Resources

A third and relatively unexpected element of pedagogic discourse relates to resources because these regulate what can be thought and realised in terms of school and classroom organisation, including pupil grouping. In question and answer sessions, Bernstein was frequently asked how and whether the structure he described would be changed. Change, he noted, or any move to 'interrupt' the processes of social reproduction usually had time and resource implications. Some examples of what we mean by 'resource' dimensions of pedagogic discourse can only be sketched. One pertinent example is the relative spend on pupils in different age categories in the UK. Pupils in schools and colleges aged 16+, that is, students over the age of compulsory schooling, have more financial resources devoted to them, per capita, than younger secondary students who, in turn, have more spent on them than those in nursery and primary schools. Moreover, there have always also been differences in spending between LEAs, whose resources are derived both centrally and locally. However, research over 30 years has pointed to the disproportionately large social and educational benefits that accrue via high quality nursery and primary education, especially for children from least affluent backgrounds. Note also that it is children from professional and middle-class families who historically have stayed on, in disproportionate numbers, into post-compulsory education. It is true that some adjustments have been made in the direction of targeting more resources upon younger students, but the spending gap between them and post-compulsory students was still substantial. In 2001–2, for example, expenditure per pupil in primary schools was £2,620, while in secondary schools, including post-compulsory students, it was £3,210. Spend per head in higher education for the same year was £5,120 (DfES, 2004). Any re-distribution of these resources would take a supreme act of political will because it would reverse arrangements that have suited the interests of professionals and the salariat.

School and classroom organisation can be directly linked to questions of resource. Class sizes in primary and secondary schools have remained relatively stable but their reduction has been shown to have a small but important impact on student performance, especially in the early years of primary school (Blatchford *et al.*, 2003). Benefits accrued mostly to the socially disadvantaged and those whose formal schooling is conducted in a second language. Costs were high for small effect sizes. Another attempt to reduce adult-child ratios in the classroom has been through the appointment of assistants in support of qualified teachers in primary classrooms and in 2003, as part of a long running and deeply contested policy about changing pay and conditions of service, in secondary schools (Doward, 2004). Lowering infant class size in the UK in the post-1997 period under Labour, has meant reducing reception classes (at 5 years old) to less than 30 pupils per teacher which, indicatively, leaves them about twice the size of those in most of the fee-paying sector.

As Bernstein (1996) trenchantly observed, all pedagogies have costs and those that allow for variation in pacing, prerequisite to individualisation in pedagogic practice, are relatively expensive of time, teacher resource and teaching and learning materials (Al-Ramahi and Davies, 2002). Resources represent the hierarchy of interests that is external to the school. The level and distribution of finance to categories of students means that traditional forms of organisation, classroom interaction and pedagogical practice remain in place, as do the outputs that flow from the system.

Conclusion

In this chapter we have sought to explain how 'gaps' in attainment, conventionally measured by school examinations have been maintained and reproduced. We have looked at Bernstein's early work to show that explanations have long been available that show that we require a sociologically rich and complex framework if we are to understand the structure and processes of social reproduction. We have stressed that each of the sites that compose the 'triad' family, school and work, carries on the work of intergenerational transmission and, thus, the allocation of who gets what. Unlike social mobility theorists, we do not contend that education 'mediates' the relationships between the family (origin) and the division of labour (destination). Education's social function is as a form of identity work whose generating principle is to sift and sort students predominantly by what is defined and measured as ability. We argued it is a domain where there is an embedded 'constellation of orientations', defined in pedagogic discourse, that are selectively transmitted and acquired. We also noted that privileged students, those with an extended experience of specific forms of linguistic, cognitive and social interaction, particularly to certain modes of control, have structures of perceptions that inform their successful navigation of schools' constellation of meanings and message systems. These are, to a large degree, acquired tacitly, outside education's domain but actualised within the privileging practices of the school. In Hasan's (2004: 41) terms, referring to Vygotsky's (1978: 84) dictum that '(A)ny learning a child encounters in school has a previous history', developing 'shaped mind' further or in different directions 'will be a difficult goal to achieve if we go on assuming homogeneity of coding orientations for all pupils and the myth of egalitarian education'.

Attention was devoted to what Bernstein denoted as 'pedagogic discourse', the durable ensemble of meanings, orientations and practices that compose the field of education, created in official pedagogic discourse but appropriated by other subordinate discursive levels and relayed, more or less circuitously from central state to schools and classrooms. Our argument is that this durable ensemble composed of three principles or orientations concerning sifting and sorting, privileging practices and resources has proved somewhat impervious to attempts via education policy to substantive re-writing and reform. Over the period of time that has been our focus in the last five chapters we suggest that education policy has had effects on school organisation but little real effect on the social function of schools, whose fundamental features in these respects have changed only at the margins. Moreover, the principles upon which they are conducted, the recognition, realisation and reward of specific modes of language, perception and control, have also remained stable. We should stress that schools and teachers are not acting arbitrarily here. Schools reflect the importance and value placed on them from outside and it is a question for debate as to whether, echoing Castells (1996, 1997, 1998) and Tyler (2004: 27) it is right in suggesting that, in the information age, 'pedagogic relations assume a new and constitutive status'.

7 Something happened
The policy framework post-1988

Introduction

The recent narrative history of British education can be organised around two landmark pieces of legislation. The first, the 1944 Education Act has been referred to extensively in earlier chapters of this book. It is the 1988 Education Reform Act (ERA, 1988) that now provides the additional lynch pin of the policy framework that governs the structure and processes of British education. The idea of framework is appropriate because the new rules and arrangements have already extended across four administrations, two Conservative and two Labour governed, as a reading of Skocpol (1992) might lead us to expect. The ERA, 1988 and associated legislation was assembled around a set of principles some of which were very different from those that underpinned the 1944 Act and, indeed, aimed to address what were thought to be some of the shortcomings of the earlier legislation and policy framework. One key theme of the legislation was to assert greater central state authority, further rewriting the balance of power and control between it and local government authorities. The 1988 framework was also distinctive because it was created by a Conservative Party sheltering a variety of interests, including industrial trainers and cultural restorationists under its strong, neo-liberal wing (Ball, 1990), already busy with the introduction of the TVEI, perceiving itself to have a clear electoral mandate to reinvent principles of public sector service provision on 'new management' or private sector principles, including education. That has been strongly reflected in the attempt to create markets in education and expand the right of parents to express a preference in the selection of schools for their children. In this chapter we shall consider each of these themes in turn and their implications for British education and its wider social functions.

Centralisation: reasserting central authority, putting on the pressure

We have suggested that, by the mid-1960s, central governments showed a greater willingness to influence the local organisation of schools but curriculum and pedagogy were still considered to be the responsibility of LEAs, schools and educational professionals. We have also argued that Labour Prime Minister

Callaghan's iconic speech at Ruskin College in 1976, was an event that signalled the direction change was likely to take (Kogan, 2002; Phillips, 2001). He called attention to the wider social functions of education and noted that it had to be responsive to the demands of a changing economy, a restructured labour market and the needs of employers. The curriculum was no longer to be regarded as 'the secret garden' tended exclusively by educational professionals. This and associated events, like the Great Debate orchestrated by his Education Secretary, Shirley Williams, created public and official climates for the radical changes in the policy-making that began under a neo-liberal Conservative government in 1979. Between then and 1988, little attempt was made to consult with teachers, LEAs or bodies and organisations, such as the Schools' Council (disbanded in 1984) which had once provided them with a voice among policy makers. They were seen as 'part of the problem', 'producer interests' that acted as barriers to the creation of system designed to 'raise standards' in education. ERA, 1988 represented the Conservative government's ideological preferences and commitment towards culturally conservative school knowledge that, apart from the 'nationalisation' of the curriculum that it entailed, pleased cultural restorationists (Fitz *et al.*, 1993). The centre pieces of the Act, the establishment of a National Curriculum and the creation of local educational markets rolled back the 1944 principle of locally controlled public services in favour of the subordination of LEAs, schools and educational professionals to central agendas in terms of curriculum, pedagogy and assessment. At the same time, and without apparent avowal of paradox, schools were recast as individual cost centres and were given greater control over their internal operations and, to some degree, exposed to competitive educational quasi-markets. The concomitant loss of function of LEAs that was entailed put schools into more direct relationship with central government and its official agents so that apparent greater decentralisation led to its contrary.

The process of centralisation has been symbolised by successive alteration in the shape and name of the central department of state and refined by increasing the number and capacities of the official recontextualising agents that surrounded it. The primary task of this new ensemble has been to regulate the various activities of LEAs, schools and educational professionals. Its main features flowed as results of policies developed by successive Conservative administrations between 1979–97. Since the election of the first 'new' Labour government in 1997, the main thrust of centralisation has not only been maintained but expanded, as a realigned Left has vied for the support of the same groups in the electorate that it perceived had approved of the post-1988 arrangements. Within central government and notably under Blair's Labour administration (though the reality of such direct intervention in education was established by Thatcher), formal prominence has been accorded to the coordinating role of the Prime Minister whose policy unit now ranks in influence alongside that of the Education Secretary and civil servants in the department of state in the governance of education. At the heart of the centralisation process, however, has been the creation of a meso-state; largely composed of quangos, non-elected, ministeriallyappointed agencies, responsible for the provision of aspects of education, social and welfare services. They are accountable upwards to ministers but have no clear lines of accountability downwards to citizens and electors. In education, for example, teacher training is regulated in England by the Teacher Training Agency (TTA) (though it is regulated by the Welsh Assembly Government (WAG) in Wales), while the Qualifications and Curriculum and Authority (QCA) (known as Awdurdod Cymwysterau Cwricwlwm ac Asesu Cymru (ACCAC) in Wales) monitors the National Curriculum (NC) and the national testing of students. Non-ministerial departments, the Office for Standards in Education (OFSTED) in England and Estyn in Wales, operating through contracted, registered, private inspection teams, are the agencies responsible for the inspection of LEAs, schools and teacher education.

All these agencies have important functions in policymaking arenas. LEAs, in policy terms once important partners, now act primarily not even as recontextualisers but reproducers of central policy, alongside schools. Within policy making arenas they are no longer seen as serous players. In the discourse of our time they are 'deliverers' of the curriculum and other policies, with few minor watchdog functions with respect of schools. The central state has established a formidable institutional complex with which to regulate curriculum and pedagogic practices in schools. In England and Wales these have come to include:

1   a NC composed of three 'core' subjects and seven 'foundation' subjects (eight in Wales, including Welsh), each initially devised by a specialist, handpicked panel and modified on a number of occasions since, which all maintained schools are required to teach. In addition there are associated testing procedures, in which children undertake end of Key Stage national tests at ages 7, 11, 14 and GCSE at 16. Followed by the publication of examination performance 'league' tables for all schools in England, except at Key Stage 1 (7-year-olds). Wales has recently abandoned national tests for 7-year-olds and is set to abandon tests for 11- and 14-year-olds. It has also ceased to publish league tables. If Thatcher's intention in introducing the NC was to (re)introduce order and conformity in school subjects, the version of testing devised by the Task Group on Assessment and Testing (TGAT) that she accepted was considerably more complex than she had initially thought necessary. For her, tests that established a simple, paper and pencil metric which parents could use in shopping for schools would have sufficed. The tests were officially justified on the basis that they would sensitively measure children's level of achievement and supply a better understanding of which would contribute to raising standards. But they also functioned to ensure that schools adhered to the NC core. In retrospect, as we shall see, they have also served to narrow the remainder of the primary and, to a lesser degree, secondary curriculum;

2   inspection, on an initial 4-year cycle in England and a 5-year cycle in Wales by semi-privatised inspectorates, against published criteria by OFSTED in England and Estyn in Wales, both led by the old HMI cadres. The cycle of

inspection has become differentiated with less frequent, more 'light touch' events aimed at schools whose results suggest they are doing well, as measured by conventional indicators. Inspection reports are available to parents. Schools under this system can be declared to be 'failing' and, if necessary, taken over and put into the Fresh Start programme under which existing teaching staff are dismissed. They are required to apply for their former posts in the newly named and constituted schools. Similar procedures were also applied to LEAs;

3   national literacy and numeracy strategies introduced into 20,000 primary schools in 1998 that required all primary schools in England to devote one hour each day to teaching literacy and another hour to numeracy. These hours were to follow a prescribed formula of whole class teaching, group and individual work. Wales has not adopted the prescribed 'hours' though the published material and practices that defined them have been widely followed;

4   a 'national curriculum' for teacher education, foreshadowed from 1984 in the work of Council for the Accreditation of Teacher Education (CATE), devised by the TTA after 1992 but bearing the marks of ministerial predilections specified, among other things, length of training, period of school based practice, the levels of grammatical and numerical competence required by intending teachers as well as a demonstrated ability in the management of 'whole class' teaching (Carvel, 1997b; Gardiner, 1997; Furlong, 2001);

5   target setting for schools and LEAs, a Labour government initiative that set levels of attainment for each school and local authority expressed in terms of the percentages of pupils achieving specified grades. Persistent under-performance was likely to trigger the interest of school inspectorates. Targets were also linked to;

6   performance-related pay for teachers, whose official designation was 'threshold payments'. Individual teachers have been required to apply to be assessed against a basket of centrally generated criteria, including their students' performance; and

7   involvement of educational entrepreneurs' located in commercial businesses, not-for-profit organisations and universities in the take over of schools and LEAs, the provision of school improvement and school effectiveness advice plus school and staff development programmes for LEAs and schools. As this service has grown, the role and scale of LEA inspection and advice units have been even further diminished.

The grip that the centre has taken on the system has been justified as action necessary to drive up standards. Its emphases on what Ball (2000) has anatomised as 'performativity' demonstrated a lack of confidence in the abilities or willingness of LEAs and educationists to contribute otherwise to policy goals. The accumulation of performance indicators, targets and interventions, on the one hand and punitive initiatives, on the other, showed in the starkest terms where power now resided. Much of its analysis in detail would require entry to myriad advisory and executive groups, much given to secrecy and spin. These policies have also cumulatively redefined pedagogic authority. The proliferation of what Bernstein (1990, 1996), termed official pedagogic recontextualising agencies, such as the TTA, QCA and OFSTED, each concerned with a specific domain of education policy and practice, has created powerful mechanisms through which to project and monitor specific discourses of teaching and learning. One only has to think of primary school teachers and the language through which they describe and discuss their colleagues and children in their classes to appreciate the reorientation that the NC, its testing and the requirements of some of the agencies referred to above have become embedded in schools. 'Meet Jenny, she teaches KS 2, Kate is curriculum coordinator for English and James is our SENCO (special educational needs coordinator)' is now an entirely understood technical language installed only since 1988. Alongside this we have: 'Ahmed is KS1, Mary over there is level three in science, about a level above him and progressing at well above the class average'. It is a language of description mapping out children's progress and achievement, again in terms that have their origins in 1988. Students in initial teacher training learn no different, experienced teachers are re-socialised into new ways and vocabularies, though a significant number in the period running up to and in the first flush of post-1988 implementation 'resisted' by resigning or retiring.

At the same time there has been, as one might expect, strong evidence that educational professionals have challenged, subverted and adapted centrally generated curriculum and pedagogic policies and have buffered students from the worst effects of the new assessment policy (Ball, 1994; Gipps *et al.*, 1995; Pollard *et al.*, 1994). Nevertheless, theirs has been primarily a response that has been required to accept an agenda and dominant official discourse emanating from the centre. The wider implications of this intensified central regulation were to be found in the range of educational identities projected in its combination of curriculum, pedagogic and inspection policies. In general terms, the educational identities constructed in and through the NC, the inspection process and pedagogic guidance corresponded with those that Bernstein (1996: 76) called 'retrospective [...] constructed from grand narratives, cultural and religious, recontextualized to stabilise a past in the future, their collective base more important than their exchange value'. The subject-based curriculum, the insistence that Shakespeare and other writers in the 'canon' be taught in NC English, that history should be about statecraft and the dissemination of British traditions, the requirement that schools be inspected to establish the state of students' spiritual, social, moral and cultural development (evidence of which, in part, will be a daily collective act of religious worship, broadly Christian in character) and a firm steer towards strong framing in classrooms all pointed to attempted revitalisation of nationalism and traditionalism to be embedded in student identities. Alongside this, however, governments have attempted to foster modernisation via the inclusion of technology as a NC subject and has invited schools to adopt a technology focus through the National Grid for Learning

(Selwyn and Fitz, 2001), as well as encouraging technology and specialist schools (Fitz *et al.*, 1993; Gorard *et al.*, 2003). In this respect it has provided schools with opportunities to specialise and to devise alternative futures. We would add that none of the features of the NC or its modernisation is inimical to the interests and ambitions of professional and middle-class families. Indeed, as Bernstein noted 30 years ago, the strong preference, particularly of the new middle class, was for primary classrooms where boundaries between work, play and subjects were weak and pedagogy 'invisible', aiding teacher discovery of the multiple talents of their progeny while, for secondary schools, their preferences, given that their abilities had now been made explicit, was for strong subject boundaries in traditional knowledge domains, as found in grammar schools and in the NC.

Recent Labour governments have been keenly committed not only to using the available levers created by their predecessors, but have added several of their own in order to maintain pressure on schools to improve levels of attainment. Their first White Paper, *Excellence in Schools* (DfEE, 1997) declared a 'zero tolerance' policy for under-performing LEAs, schools and teachers. That agenda has been pursued more or less unremittingly through a series of standards-driven reforms. Central government can now point to the proportion of 11-year-olds achieving benchmark standards in literacy and numeracy having risen by 19 and 20 percentage points respectively in the period 1996–2002 (Earl *et al.*, 2003). The percentage of 16-year-old students obtaining the official benchmark level of 5 GCSE grades A*–C has increased by 4 points between1996–7 and 2000–1 (Welsh Assembly Government, 2002). On this basis it has been argued that external, downward pressure and upward accountability really work and that the subordination of other stakeholders is less important than gains in student attainment. But how have these other stakeholders fared under the accountability system we outlined above?

LEAs have been squeezed and their former powers diminished in many respects, though central direction of curriculum and pedagogy has left them with marginally important school and student support functions (Firestone *et al.*, 2000; Riley and Louis, 2000; Kogan, 2002) that are primarily concerned with the 'delivery' of central initiatives. They now act more in complicity than with autonomy in: the organisation of the numeracy and literacy strategies; assisting and advising schools to set performance targets; providing guidance to schools in order for them to meet the objectives set out in school inspection reports; and through offering schools a menu of in-service professional development activities. Schools as budget holders, however, can choose whether to purchase their continuing professional development services from LEAs or from other agencies so that, in many respects, a strong customer-client relationship now exists between LEAs and 'their' schools rather than one characterised by regulative paternalism, colleagueship and respect. Former advisory and inspection units are now expected to be virtually self-funding, as in one LEA we visited, typically covering only 20 per cent of the unit's costs, the rest earned by commercial provision of services and staff development to local schools. Their second key role, as planners, providers and organisers of local schools has been seriously undermined by choice and diversity policies, whose implications we discuss in the next section.

The organisational imperative in both primary and secondary schools has become to maximise levels of student performance in national assessments (Gillborn and Youdell, 1999; Jeffrey, 2002). In response, as we noted in Chapter 4, many secondary schools have been inclined to re-introduce more homogeneous forms of ability grouping in the early years of high school (Fitz *et al.*, 2000) as well as measures to identify students at the threshold of achieving C and D grades in GCSE classes (15–16-year-olds), putting in extra resources to maximise their chances of obtaining the C grades or better that are the official basis of schools' standing (Gillborn and Youdell, 1999). Primary schools have also been subjected to similar kinds of pressures (Pollard *et al.*, 1994; Croll, 1996; Galton, 1999), tending to have less control over what is taught and its sequencing and pacing than prior to the introduction of the National Curriculum. While Alexander (1997) has argued that there has been considerable continuity in the amount of time that primary schools have tended to spend on 'the basics' before and after the NC, Galton (1999) reported that, in order to teach the ten NC subjects, one early effect in primary schools was a reduction in the time devoted to literacy and numeracy, with a subsequent decline in the standards achieved by students in these fundamental areas. The literacy and numeracy strategies have reversed those trends and lost ground made up may explain several years of rather startling increments in pupil's KS scores which Secretaries of State, no matter how hard they promise, now find it difficult to keep up. But time in the primary school to devote to the physical and expressive side of the curriculum, in PE, art, drama and music remains unacceptably difficult to find and fund, while history and geography appear to have lost both time and place.

With respect of teachers, academic debate, informed by wider issues of the changing autonomy of the education system and changing modes of production in an increasingly globalised world, has focused on whether, and to what extent, central government interventions have led to the 'deskilling' of the profession (Croll, 1996; Jeffrey, 2002; Furlong, 2001). The most robust data we have are those which come from two major longitudinal studies of primary school teachers (Galton 1999; Galton *et al.*, 1980; Pollard *et al.*, 1994; Croll, 1996). These studies have reported a narrowing of focus in the work of teachers directed towards the interpretation and implementation of NC programmes of study rather than more creative activities where curriculum design seeks to match the particular needs of their children. There was also some indication that the NC and its associated assessments were making teachers' relationships with students less personal. While the immediate effect of the NC had led teachers in the initial study of Pollard *et al.* (1994) to feel more constrained in their professional practice, at follow-up they had redefined their professional roles and were less inclined to report feeling constricted in their practices (Croll, 1996). There was also broad acknowledgement that, since 1988, teachers' work had intensified as it was relocated, via systems of accountability, into what we have noted as a 'discourse of performativity' (Ball, 2000; Jeffrey, 2002). In it, teaching success has come to be narrowly defined in terms of efficiency and outputs, as measured by student performance in tests, meeting targets and doing well in school inspection reports. However, an alternative to England's very strong accountability system is beginning to develop in Wales where relations between schools and inspectorate have avoided the punitive character that they took for many years in England and whose General Teachers' Council has been characterised by good feeling between teacher associations and officers rather than English loggerheads. The WAG has abandoned national tests for 7-year-olds, has more collaborative and less prescriptive national literacy and numeracy strategies, no longer publishes league tables of school performance and it is refining the NC for Wales, the *Cwricwlwm Cymreig*. Although its schools and teachers are, then, monitored with a lighter touch than their English counterparts, there is no research evidence as yet on whether, to what extent, or in what direction they will employ this professional space to change or adjust their pedagogic and assessment practices.

Our account has emphasised the cumulative assertion of pedagogic authority by central government at the expense of power and control formerly exercised by stakeholders under the 1944 framework. We noted earlier that schools had gained greater independence over their internal managerial, including staffing and financial, operations. Moreover, many more secondary schools are able to determine their own admissions policies. This development has arisen in part from Conservative governments' determination to reduce the control of LEAs over schools, putatively to 'free them from the burden of bureaucrats'. In consequence, schools were required to run their own budget, planning and carrying out their expenditure accordingly. They have greater powers of hiring and firing (largely by employing more staff on short term contracts) and are freer to create their own management structures and to staff subject areas as they see appropriate and can contrive. These changes reflect the no-liberal (free market) element of the 1988 framework. Both major political parties have seen freestanding, autonomous schools as necessary components of an educational market where they might compete for students so that, apparently against the grain of other tendencies to centralisation, schools can be said to have been given greater independence. The paradox is almost certainly more apparent than real and to place this in proper context we now turn to examine the second element aspect of the 1988 framework, markets and choice in education.

Choice and diversity: power to parents?

We live in a 'market economy' and markets surround us in everything from food and drink to sex. They differ in their degrees of freedom and openness, the number and size of sellers and buyers and the quality of information that exists within them. While we tend to equate the term with private production and consumption ruled by prices and profits where buyers or consumers pay directly for goods and services, there are many things that societies decide to deliver collectively, paid for through taxation and not at the point of delivery (Lane, 1993). It is not that there is no market in these things but that decisions about production and distribution in them are made by administrative means, in terms of more or less complex sets of criteria about what should be made available, to whom and on what terms. These decisions are political and delivery of goods and services may be in the hands of public servants or private contractors. The list is very large, from national defence and policing, to household rubbish collection. In 'Western', post-industrial societies, more than 40 per cent of gross national product, including transfer payments, such as social security entitlements, passes through the state, either as direct production, taxation or charges of one form or another (Twine, 1994), Different societies and communities draw the line at different points between public (or social) and private goods and their production, pricing and availability. In Britain, health services are largely 'free' at the point of delivery, but in the USA they are not. In most countries, state produced, 'public' education is basically both free and compulsory, though parents may chose to educate their children privately. Free, nationalised education is a relatively new phenomenon, dating back only to the end of the nineteenth century in the British elementary school system and stuttering into being at the secondary level until the coming of the 1944 Act (Simon, 1948; Lawson and Silver, 1973). It has always coexisted with private or fee-paying education whose extent, as we saw in Chapter 4, varies sharply, even between the countries that make up Britain, though its power and social significance are hard to overestimate. Moreover, there are complex shadings of private and public, not least in higher education, of which we have made little mention, for example, in the huge income from endowments of most Oxbridge colleges, whose distinction from the rest of the system has been further marked by government double funding, increased 'international' student fees and their increasing orientation toward commercial exploitation of research and knowledge transfer. Indeed, we appear to be on the brink of producing an even more deeply divided and privatised British higher education system with college President talk (Ward, 2004, quoting Beloff of Trinity College, Oxford) of government tanks on their lawns, ready to enforce lower-class intake targets ('a scary vision of students from "bog standard comprehensives" proceeding to "Mickey Mouse degrees"') in exchange for the first step in allowing student fees to rise toward market rates. Only an impercipience of vice-chancellors could possibly imagine that the regime of bursaries and scholarships required in exchange could lead to more egalitarian entry patterns or leave more than a few of their institutions better off.

There have, then, long been markets in education, both private and public. The struggle for control of their criteria or rules, for what Bernstein (1990, 1996) called 'the pedagogic device', concerning what public education should be made available by whom to whom and on what terms, is the very stuff of sociological and policy study. It requires a cool head in a deeply ideological field for, quite apart from those who argue blindly or self interestedly that payment at the point of delivery is the ultimate good or enemy, either with respect of efficiency, social justice or morality, there are serious questions both about the intimacy of the relation between market codes and wider freedoms and the social impact of private and collective pursuits of interest. Debate is frequently far from 'innocent'. Empirical likelihood and interests intertwine, that is to say, ideology is everywhere. When discourse turns to markets and choice we need to locate it immediately in unequal, ongoing arrangements.

What has been referred to as a policy of deliberate extension of market forces in education in the UK commenced almost as soon as the Conservative government took office in 1979 and arrangements assumed their shape over the next decade (Bowe *et al.*, 1992). It involved the creation of interlocking policy initiatives aimed at forcing some degree of competition between schools and increasing parental choice. The institutional policy instruments employed in market creation have been discussed fully elsewhere (e.g. Whitty *et al.*, 1998; Fitz *et al.*, 1993; Grubb and Finkelstein, 2000). Briefly, in England and Wales a 'limited market' at the school level was created and advanced by the policy initiatives outlined below:

1   an *Assisted Places Scheme*, started in 1981, aimed to provide financial support of students from families of modest means to attend fee-paying schools deemed to be academically excellent. This did not introduce a new principle but extended an old principle whereby LEAs had formerly paid for some students to attend private institutions;

2   *reformed governing bodies*, introduced in 1986 and consolidated in 1988, involving reduction in LEAs and increased parental and business community representation;

3   plans for *City Technology Colleges* (CTCs), announced in 1986. Initiatives were to be invited for schools to bid for funding to specialise in maths, technology and later, languages, performing arts and sport. These were outside the control of LEAs, funded in partnership between government and private enterprise, the former meeting recurrent costs;

4   *grant-maintained (GM) schools*, introduced in 1988, enabling schools to opt out or leave the control of their LEA after a successful ballot of parents and receive funding directly from central government;

5   *local management of schools* (LMS), part of the 1988 legislation, devolved financial and management responsibilities to schools. Each school was to be formula funded, 80 per cent of which was based on an age weighted, per capita formula; and

6   *open enrolment* also arose from the 1988 legislation, enabling schools to recruit up to their physical capacity and, following the so-called Greenwich judgement in the same year, allowing parents to select schools outside the administrative boundaries of their own LEA, thus undermining local planning and neighbourhood school policies (see Whitty, 1995; Maclure, 1989).

What were the wider intentions and implications of these initiatives? Open enrolment entailed that parents could express a preference for their child to attend any school with surplus places (Fitz *et al.*, 2002b). More importantly, linked to a per capita funding regime where the number of students attending a school, not social or educational needs, determined its share of the local budget, any loss in student numbers would mean year-on-year reduction in its financial resources and vice versa, rather than change buffered by local administrative judgement. Schools were effectively put under pressure to maintain their 'market share' of students. With GM schools at the same time 'opting out' of LEAs to receive funding directly from central government, the cumulative effect of these policies was to transfer many LEA functions to schools and parents. Birth rate changes and population movement had always required LEAs to plan for changes in provision. Now often longstanding plans to amalgamate, re-designate or close schools in order to reduce surplus places were disrupted by schools opting out or threatening to do so to avoid such fates befalling them. In Wales the very few cases of 'opting out' that occurred were regarded as being on the part of shrinking schools anxious to avoid closure. The most striking trend, however, was the determination of the very great majority of grammar schools, comprising four per cent of all secondaries in England, to become grant-maintained. They preserved overt, selective admission policies in the face of LEAs, such as Gloucestershire, that had progressively attempted to become fully comprehensive (Fitz *et al.*, 2002a).

In short, these policies were intended to change or at least challenge nation-wide systems of allocation of students to places by LEAs, based largely on locally defined neighbourhood or catchment areas and with a minimum of overt selection, by ones where parents exercised 'choice' in local 'markets' featuring a 'diversity' of schools. The Education Act, 1980 had formally established the parental right to a voice in the allocation of school places to their children (Commission for Racial Equality, 1983) and created the Assisted Places Scheme whose public justification, though not necessarily chief effect, was to allow able children from poor families to attend fee-paying schools (Edwards *et al.*, 1989). This legislative trend towards explicit parental preference continued with the Education Reform Act, 1988, the Parents' Charter, 1991 and the subsequent White Paper in 1992 (Jowett, 1995). However, by the early 1990s, despite such transfer of power to schools and parents, it was still LEAs which generally determined the rules for admission where demand exceeded capacity but only among the schools still in their control. At the same time, whatever the legislation in force, both schools and authorities had always had considerable leeway in terms of its interpretation and application. In the late 1980s for example, CTCs, outside the control of the LEAs within which they were located, were charged explicitly to follow criteria for the allocation of their limited places, particularly with respect of their intakes being 'representative of the community they serve'. In practice, researchers found considerable variation between colleges as to how these criteria were applied (Murphy *et al.*, 1990). Voluntary aided schools, with governor majorities appointed by their (usually) religious foundations, entitled to determine admissions, showed substantial differences in their policies. While this was not new, added to the effect of essentially privatised GM (now Foundation, with those still maintained by the LEA renamed Community) schools applying their own selection procedures for a significant proportion of their intake and CTCs' subversion of their criteria of entry, the picture of school allocation, despite continuingly relatively prescriptive national legislation, had become very complex.

In some areas, the proportion of secondary schools falling into these categories has seen LEA functions amalgamated with those of other departments, such as social services. In others, like Kingston and Richmond, student traffic in and out of their secondary 'systems' (though again not a new phenomenon) became very heavy. In Wandsworth and elsewhere, families were faced with a bewildering array of secondary school entry procedures whose successful navigation required skills that had nothing to do with the merits of 11-year-olds. These circumstances all became part of a downward pressure on LEAs to become service agencies for schools, providing them with advice on teaching and school effectiveness measures on a commercial basis, in a system where popular ('good', 'strong') schools prospered and expanded, unpopular ('bad', 'weak') schools moved through 'special measures' to renewal, sometimes involving privatisation or closure. Overt school accountability to parents as consumers was increased by the publication of school inspection reports, league tables of student attainment in national tests and public examinations and student attendance rates. How parents have made sense or use of them has always been constrained by the lack of 'value added' data, meaning that they are best viewed as school input rather than output measures. A shortage of available places in 'popular' ones, as well as the socio-cultural resources available to them has been the focus of a series of important studies by Stephen Ball and his associates. He saw the issue as part of:

> the search for new methods of welfare funding and welfare delivery, and the attempt to ensure and retain the commitment of the middle class to the state provision of welfare services. The politics of choice is a key element in this retention [...] the interests of the state and those of the middle class come together in the relation between positional advantage and the state's fostering of international economic competitiveness [...] Choice policies [...] in the current socio-economic context, are an effective response to the interest anxieties of the middle class.
>
> (Ball, 2003: 30)

It is clear from his and others' work that the policy intent of Conservative governments over seventeen years to put schools into the orbit of parental preferences has been warmly embraced by Labour governments since 1997. Historic planning and providing powers of LEAs, especially their control over school admissions policies, have been further diminished by their determination to 'diversify' the system of secondary education mainly by seizing on and expanding what is now known as the 'specialist schools' programme. By the end of the current year it was aimed to have about 30 per cent of all secondary schools in England designated as 'specialist' (Gorard and Taylor, 2001). Fears have been expressed that this 'diversity' will become the basis of a new two-tier system of provision where specialist schools, with advantages of increased funding and control over their admissions, recruit increasingly socio-economically privileged intakes. We will discuss this in greater detail in the next chapter.

Schools have also been able to bid to central government for extra resources under other initiatives. The Education Action Zone (EAZ) initiative was an area-based policy designed to target resources at disadvantaged communities (Gewirtz, 1999). A zone included one or two secondary schools and designated primary schools working together under a director and guided by a 'forum' of parents, educational and local community and business representatives. Once more, LEAs were marginalised by their funding arrangements as well as, in the case of specialist schools, being left out of determining admissions arrangements. What has also been significant in these policies is Labour's determination to fund them via public–private coalitions. Applicant specialist schools and EAZs had to show they had raised sums or had promises, in cash or kind, in the case of specialist schools of £50,000 or more, in order to attract matching grants from central government. How much hard cash has actually been raised from the private sector is difficult to judge but it has proved less than easy for many applicants to put together the funding required. The EAZ initiative has been terminated primarily because no clear connection could be made between the policy and its anticipated impact on raising levels of student achievement. Focus on inner urban and other disadvantaged communities has remained, however, supported via the Excellence in Cites programme and an expansion of what are called 'city academies', based on what has become Labour's educational *leitmotif*, the partnership between private sector sponsors and central government funding. These will also be discussed in more detail in the next chapter.

With respect of choice, Wales has pulled away from England in a number of respects. It has sustained and promoted a secondary school system based on all-ability comprehensive schools with no selective grammar schools. It has neither adopted the specialist schools programme nor introduced EAZs. It has, at the same time, been otherwise preoccupied with the development of Welsh medium and bilingual provision, whose complex shape and incidence appear to reflect both the distribution and strengths of aspirant and actual Welsh speaking communities and class choice. Empirical data are scarce (see Heath, 2000). WAG's intention has been to create a system of choice between community-based schools broadly similar in character, though its urban schools show no sign of converging in terms of their intake characteristics (see Chapter 9).

One further broad trend in recent educational (and other public services) initiatives in England, and elsewhere in the UK, based on public–private partnerships has been the Private Finance Initiative (PFI) where funding of new schools and the refurbishment of others involves financial consortia undertaking building projects that are then leased back to LEAs for a substantial fee over a 30-year period (Fitz and Beers, 2002). While it is clear that PFI's popularity with Chancellors of the Exchequer anxious to transfer capital to current expenditure is the secret of its success, making it partly the creature of old British Treasury habits, as well as European Commission convergence rules, it constitutes a huge swing in preference to outsourcing and against the competence of central and local government planners and professionals The apparent paradox of Labour governments pursuing such a course has not gone un-noticed and such policies have been interpreted as representing progressive privatisation of public education (Hatcher, 1998). There are two sets of accountability issues raised here. The first relates to the commercialisation of education and the implications that has for the character of a public service and ultimately for student identities. The second relates to questions of who owns and controls schools for, under PFI arrangements, they have to negotiate with sponsors when and how buildings will be used for other, possibly non-educational, purposes. It may also be the case that PFIs require maintenance staff contracts to move from schools to their private sponsors. Thus far few schools have been privatised in this way but a strong framework now exists that would enable many more to be taken over by private, commercial and not for profit organisations. These trends will also be discussed in more detail in Chapter 9.

Conclusion

Developments in educational policy over the last three decades have reposi-tioned three key agents, central government, LEAs and educational profes-sionals in new relations of power and control. In general, this has involved transfers of authority from and subordination of LEAs and professionals to central government in response to the latter's much more active policy preferences. We have come a very long way, from the immediate post-Second World War era when central government neither thought that it could nor wished to specify and control the state system other than in terms of its broad character, where Education Minister George Tomlinson could with justice claim that 'Minister knows 'owt about curriculum', to one where its inter-ventions are direct and detailed, though only marginally based on public consultation or research. Education is no longer regarded, in the rhetoric, as being 'outside politics', that is to say, a matter of cross-party consensus, but deeply involved in electoral politics. Paradoxically, as much of our account has exemplified, this does not mean that the parties are deeply divided on policy, on the contrary, they have strongly converged in key areas. The explanations most readily to hand as to why this has been the case seem to be twofold. First, they lie in the need for politicians to quell the 'interest anxieties' of middle-class groups whose votes are pivotal to their prospect of office. Second, globalisation of the world economy has inscribed 'must not fall behind, must compete' in all their hearts. Britain must be (another little paradox) a high skill, low employment-cost, that is to say, relatively low wage economy where educational discourse must take a different turn. Teacher and school autonomy is insulation to be stripped away, just as the economy stands more exposed and both are brought into closer relation. These issues, presaged in Bernstein (1977), we saw expressed in Chapter 7 as the prospect of a shift in pedagogic practice so as to produce more individuals with prospective, rather than retro-spective, identities. Maybe this is to be the new education divide.

In this world, unless recast as minions, LEAs, as we have seen, have been defined as standing in the way. They have kept a strategic role in raising standards in schools, each required to devise an Education Development Plan (EDP) setting out targets agreed with schools and identifying strategies for assisting in meeting them. The introduction to the National Literacy and Numeracy Strategies in England have been accompanied by increased LEA activity in supporting schools in meeting national requirements involving a limited leadership role in curriculum issues. Welsh LEAs are directly responsible for the introduction of the literacy and numeracy strategies in their schools but not on the English model of compulsion. At the same time programmes, such as EAZs, specialist schools and city academies involving public–private partnerships and direct school funding from central government have in England diminished even further their capacity, some more than others, to influence the operation of schools in their administrative boundaries. Policies, such as open enrolment, per capita funding and local management have turned schools into relatively free-standing cost centres subject to the vagaries of parental preferences and demographic changes and LEAs have very few powers to protect them from these external forces. It can be argued that schools and families have been placed in situations of 'manufactured uncertainty' (Halpin *et al.*, 1997) in competitive local education markets. In some parts of England parental fears about obtaining a place in their 'first choice' school have become so severe that a House of Commons Select Committee was convened to review current admissions policies and to make recommendations as to how to alleviate the pressures some parents now feel. One index of parental discontent is the number appealing against the decision as to which school their children have been admitted. These nearly tripled, growing from 24,573 in 1991 to 94,890 in 2001 (Education and Skills Select Committee, 2004; Fitz *et al.*, 2002a; Ward, 2004).

Schools in England and Wales have been subjected to what they initially experienced as contradictory external policy pressures on their operations that both they and we can now see as part of the same ensemble or framework of central government intentions. The first was administrative pressure which required them to conform to curriculum and assessment policies and to perform well against a number of centrally determined performance indicators. The second was pressure exerted by local educational markets within which they were required to develop strategies for institutional survival (see Woods *et al.*, 1998). Both impacted on how they were managed and led (Whitty *et al.*, 1998, Fitz *et al.*, 1997), the evidence suggesting, inevitably, that it was headteachers and their senior management teams (SMTs) that organised and took responsibility for creating institutions judged to be financially sound, administratively efficient and effective, as well as for sustaining their market share of students. Within secondary schools, subject headteachers assumed considerable responsibility for detailed interpretation and implementation of national policies on curriculum and assessment (Fitz *et al.*, 1993; Brown and Rutherford, 1998; Fitz *et al.*, 2000), subject leadership also becoming a feature of primary schools (Bell and Ritchie, 1999).

In relation to more managerially efficient and market-aware, pressured school institutions parents have been asked to bear greater personal responsibility for the choices they make about where to send their children to school. Levels of anxiety vary by region, with London being a notable hotspot (Education and Skills Committee, 2004). In the language of post-structuralism schools have become self-policing institutions, doing what is needed to survive in the market and staying below the radar of school inspectors. In political terms it looks like regulation via self-subordination. Within the same sort of language, teachers and other educational professionals can be said to have become reconstituted knowledge workers whose primary task is to 'deliver' nationally determined curricular and pedagogic strategies. Handing in a detailed weekly plan to the headteacher on the subject content to be covered and assessed for the week is a usual Monday morning expectation for primary school teachers. However, we should not underestimate the very wide scope that remains for their pedagogic and interpersonal skills in any classroom. Devising bespoke instructional and assessment programmes locally to suit judgements of the needs and capabilities of actual students in their classes has been considerably diminished. But tightness of fit of the NC straightjacket leaves considerable scope for primary and even more for secondary teachers to tailor its programmes of study to their contexts. At both levels, time, teachers' scarcest resource, has tended to become even more problematic making variation of pacing less optional. And all the while teachers have become aware of a series of performance indicators in the form of examination league tables, school inspection reports and targets that measure their relative outputs, rendering them more them both more visible and accountable to government and parents.

Labour governments have shown a surprising appetite for intervention in the operation of schools in pursuit of standards, to a degree that has exceeded previous Conservative ambitions and both parties have set education high on their electoral agendas. To the genuine surprise of many, not least its own supporters, Labour has also shown itself willing to transfer the operations of schools and LEAs officially judged to be failing to provide inadequate standards of education over to private, commercial organisations. Even where an orientation to social justice has been evident in targeting resources at socially disadvantaged communities, through policies such as EAZs, it has insisted on public–private partnerships to fund these initiatives. In these cases, public schools find themselves located within a matrix of accountability relationships; upwards to government and outwards to communities and private organisations involved directly in their governance.

One other effect of the change in the education policy framework in the direction of markets and choice has been a renewed interest in academic education policy studies. Within them, the impact of markets and choice policies on social class, access and attainment in education has been an important field of research, not least asking which existing inequalities would be made better or worse by giving parents more rights to choose a school of their choice. Advocates of choice anticipated that it would offer the opportunity to extend to socially and financially disadvantaged groups. These rights were previously enjoyed largely by financially privileged middle and professional-class families. What would be the effects of choice on social reproduction? In the next chapter we examine studies that have so far addressed the impact of choice polices on such issues.

8 Diversity
Selection and stratification

Introduction

The English secondary school system is very different from that created in 1944 in terms of its institutional variety. Tomlinson (2004) listed the following institutions: grammar, foundation (formerly GM), foundation specialist, voluntary aided, controlled faith and specialist, community (LEA controlled comprehensive), community specialist and foundation special schools, community special academies, CTCs, pupil referral units, learning support centres, Beacon (to be phased out), leading edge (to be phased in), training schools, along with Gifted and Talented Programmes. In the state maintained sector in England and Wales there were about 24,000 schools, of which approximately 4,000 were secondaries in 2004. In addition there are just over 1,500 fee-paying schools, ranging from the often long-established, predominantly boarding, major and minor 'public', through to the 'good grammar' provision of organisations like the Girls' Public School Day Trust (GPSDT) to a bewildering array of predominantly small, inexpensive and usually fundamentalist faith schools.

By no means was all of this diversity new but, as we noted in the last chapter, Conservative education policies developed in the 1980s set out to ensure that there would be a range of different schools in the state sector from which parents might choose, a policy seized upon by Labour in 1997 and carried forward with new vigour. Diversity appealed for a number of reasons. It was hoped that new kinds of school would contribute to higher standards in education by offering improved forms of curriculum and pedagogy. This has some times been expressed as 'modernising' the comprehensive principle by moving away from a 'one size fits all' system to one where some schools would act as 'beacons' to the development of adjacent schools. A further purpose, a rather residual element in a social justice agenda, has been to target resources on socio-economically disadvantaged communities by providing them with extra resources, a policy objective hitherto the province of LEAs. Diversity initiatives have generally been accompanied by provision for schools to select up to 10 per cent of their student intake on the basis of 'aptitude', a term surviving from the 1944 Act's injunction to LEAs to educate children according to their 'age, aptitude and ability'. Moreover, increasingly numerous state-funded, faith-based schools in the British context have also determined the character of their own intakes and can be seen as contributing to and sustaining 'parallel communities' where ethnic and language groups are educated in different schools (Willis, 2002: Garner, 2001). The same is broadly true of Welsh medium schools in Wales. The obvious danger here is that such diversity will exacerbate an already divided system, amounting to the re-introduction of selective education by engineering intakes so that some, often better resourced, schools are permitted to choose the most able or motivated recruits (Thornton, 2001; Hattersley, 2002).

Because the specialist schools programme has been the largest of the diversification initiatives, much of this chapter is devoted to consideration of its character and impact. Other programmes to which we shall refer have not been as extensive or well developed and general insights about the effect of diversification can best be drawn from its study. We will address only secondary school provision, though diversity policies, for example, the Beacon school programme have been extended in a limited way to state-funded primary schools. New programmes to extend school diversity by Labour governments up to 2004 have applied solely to England, so we address primarily 'English' findings though many arguments presented are still relevant to Wales and Scotland where some school diversity does exist in terms of faith-based schools and Welsh-medium schools. Furthermore, it is often reported that Welsh and Scottish local authorities, particularly in urban areas, consider features of English school diversity reforms when addressing particular educational issues. Indeed, as we noted in Chapter 6, policy and practice 'borrowing' has become part of education in a globalised age, sanctioned, not least, by decontextualised, asociological school effectiveness discourse. We focus on the organisation of school provision rather than curricular and pedagogic practices within schools. Though we are deeply concerned with the latter and acknowledge that it is the site where student identity is shaped, the brevity of this book and the relative lack of worthwhile research evidence mean that its exploration must be left to a later volume. It is, however, important to note that the cycle of policy developments in terms of within-school diversity is not in tune with development of between-school diversity.

From diversity to plurality

The 1944 Act ensured a plurality in provision, where parents were presented with a variety of different forms of secondary schooling. They were able to choose between state or private education, LEA or church, single sex or co-educational and selective or non-selective schools, though not all parents had had the same degree of choice. Parents in Wales were also increasingly able to choose between Welsh- and English-medium schools. Most of this array had existed prior to 1944, particularly selective faith-based, private fee-paying and philanthropic schools (Taylor, 2002). However, the 1944 Education Act not only signified the introduction of compulsory secondary schooling but constituted the first state attempt at purposively providing diverse secondary school provision in the form of the bi- or tripartite arrangements (see Chapters 2 and 3) including grammar schools, technical schools and modern schools. Faith schools, most of which were Church of England or Roman Catholic in affiliation, assumed 'voluntary' status and, becoming part of the state system, received state funding in exchange for LEA participation on their governing bodies. All were meant to cross social class boundaries and enjoy parity of prestige but middle-class families were typically over-represented in selective grammar schools (see Chapters 4 and 5) (Floud and Halsey, 1961; Halsey *et al.*, 1980; Silver, 1973).

The comprehensive schools that existed by the 1960s had among themselves institutions with the least degree of formal and others with a high degree of actual diversification depending, not least, on how effectively they were 'creamed' by remaining grammar schools or whether, if formed by amalgamation, they had a dominant ex-grammar school in the 'mix', keen to retain its ethos and reputation among local communities (Kerkchoff *et al.*, 1996). The commitment of local education authorities to the comprehensive 'movement' and the association between new residential development, urbanisation and new comprehensive schools varied (Taylor and Gorard, 2001). In short, the way in which comprehensive schools were accommodated into existing education landscapes that might also include religious, modern, technical, grammar and ex-grammar schools (Benn and Chitty, 1996) almost defied generalisation. By the mid-1990s, about 92 per cent of all state secondary students in England, approximately 95 per cent in Scotland and over 98 per cent in Wales attended them (Benn and Chitty, 1996), admitted predominantly by catchment areas defined largely by LEAs to encourage families to use their nearest school. Nevertheless, even prior to 1988, particularly in urban areas, parents might enjoy a considerable measure of choice, even in left-leaning LEAs, such as the Inner London Education Authority, between different types of state schools (Hargreaves, 1996).

Therefore, the neo-liberal policy framework of the 1980 and 1988 Education Acts and subsequent Conservative government legislation calling for school diversity might be seen as signifying not the first but a third 'diversity' policy phase, following the immediate post-1944 arrangements and the following 'comprehensive' phase. It was now seen as a key element in the construction of quasi-markets in education by creating state schools outside the control of LEAs, giving parents choices between LEA and self-governing schools. The CTC programme from 1986 represented the first move in this direction, establishing a pattern for the creation of different kinds of state schools, much of which is evident in today's specialist schools, which are subject-distinctive, state–private partnerships involving sponsors initially conceived of as providing sites and buildings, outside the control of LEAs, receiving government grants to support recurrent costs, with additional support from industry contributing to technology aspects of the curriculum. As the policy unfolded it became increasingly clear that its intentions were not being fully met. The involvement of private sector sponsors fell well short of expectations (Whitty *et al.*, 1993).

The GM schools initiative was a central feature of the 1988 Education Reform Act that enabled schools, after a ballot of parents, to opt out of LEA control and achieve a greater measure of autonomy, receiving funding directly from central government (Fitz *et al.*, 1993). A subsequent consultative Green Paper, *Choice and Diversity in Education* (DFE, 1992) led to new legislation and the Technology Schools Initiative allowing GM and voluntary schools to apply for technology school status, initially in science, technology, language and sports and receive substantial grants to develop their specialisms and to select up to 10 per cent of their intake by aptitude or ability. The perils of devolving admissions policies to GM schools became apparent in the mid-1990s, especially in the Greater London area and South East England, where it became increasingly difficult for parents in some LEAs to obtain places in nearby, high performing secondary schools (Fitz *et al.*, 2002a). These difficulties were most intense in areas with high concentrations of GM schools (Taylor *et al.*, 2002). It became borne in that the characteristics of such 'diversity' were very different from those of the period of school plurality where school type was the key feature in promoting diversity. A useful framework for considering these other features of school diversity altogether was provided by Bradford's (1995) private–state continuum in educational provision. This conceived school diversity as the blurring of private and public functions of education provision. Taylor (2001a: 380) took this further by considering the geographical variation in school diversity during this 'third' policy phase, arguing that different levels were achieved in different areas, reflecting 'how recent education legislation has impacted differentially across England, creating a mosaic of education markets, each one offering a different choice and constraints for parents in the market place'. As we noted in Chapter 7, this privileging of diversity and choice reflected a growing resistance to universalism in general welfare provision. We may also see it as reflecting, to some extent, a realisation that the comprehensive era retained and created serious social inequalities in education provision and outcomes.

'New' Labour and school diversity

Since 1997 Labour governments appear to have continued the neo-liberal agenda of previous Conservative governments adding a sprinkling of Anthony Giddens' 'third way' (Power and Whitty, 1999). Paterson (2003) has identified three educational ideologies underpinning their reforms: a 'New Labourism' that combined a reinterpretation of nineteenth-century liberalism with some New Right issues of the 1980s; 'developmentalism', seeking state policies to promote the competitiveness of the UK in the global market economy; and 'New Social Democracy' encompassing the benefits of the free market, with governmental intervention to limit its social consequences and recognising the importance of redistributing power, wealth and opportunity and promoting citizenship and social responsibility. Paterson contended that their policy marked a further phase in the development of school diversity reforms. We should also note how Labour's declared policy of zero tolerance for underachieving schools, complete with a militarised discourse for their liberation (failing headteachers might be 'taken out', replacement leaders 'parachuted in', and so forth), has given rise to an unprecedented willingness, via the mechanism of school inspections, to pass control of 'failing' schools and LEAs to commercial and not-for-profit agencies, extending educational privatisation (Fitz and Beers, 2002).

The early years

For many traditional Labour supporters the ending of academic selection was seen as the priority for reform. However, as Webster and Parsons (1999) have argued, ruling members of the Labour Party were not consistent on this matter focusing, rather, on the Conservative governments' 'obsession with school structures' and heralding 'standards more than structures' as the new key to success. In the words of their manifesto, Labour would 'never put dogma before children's education' (The Labour Party, 1997). Their 'standards not structures' agenda was presented as focusing, with non-ideological pragmatism, rather than what were perceived to be 'old-fashioned' arguments, upon selection. Unsurprisingly, when elected into office in 1997 their attempts to end academic selection were more rhetorical than real. The fate of the remaining 160 or so grammar schools, for example, was to be determined by parental ballot the terms of which were heavily weighted against objectors, rather than by any concerted central government effort to close them.

However, a few other early reforms did appear to represent a shift away from educational diversity towards greater homogeneity. For example, the Assisted Places Scheme that had enabled supposedly academically able children from disadvantaged backgrounds to attend fee-paying private schools was phased out and the funds saved were to be used to reduce class sizes in primary schools. A 1997 White Paper proposed the abolition of GM schools but the legislation that followed in 1998 instead revised the way in which schools were to be governed and grouped into 'community schools' (schools under LEA control), voluntary aided schools (in the main, faith-based schools) and 'foundation schools' (the great majority being former GM schools) (White *et al.*, 2001). This formally acknowledged plurality within the state education system and maintained the autonomy of VA and former GM schools on admissions policies. The White Paper had also announced the intention to embrace 'partnerships' with private and non-governmental organisations whenever these would prove to be beneficial. It not only accepted the continued existence of CTCs as independent state-funded education institutions but the model was to inform further initiatives, such as EAZs and, later, city academies.

The 1998 School Standards and Framework Act extolled the virtues of 'standards not structures' and attempted to harmonise the increasingly frustrating admission processes that emerged from previous policies to accommodate open enrolment via codes of practice, admission forums and the Office of the Schools Adjudicator (Fitz *et al.*, 2002; Taylor *et al.*, 2002). It also initiated a new programme of school diversity with the continued expansion of specialist schools and the establishment of Beacon schools. But it was the 2001 White Paper *Schools Achieving Success* and the more recent DfES (2003b) strategy document *A New Specialist System: Transforming Secondary Education*, in which the promotion of greater school diversity was made more explicit. A School Diversity Unit was created within the DfES whose primary responsibility was to encourage and investigate greater school diversity. As well as encouraging foundation and VA schools to expand in number it gestated Beacon specialist and training schools, federations, and Leading Edge Partnership schools and, most recently, city academies. This might seem ironic, given its very early focus on standards rather than structures, that not so 'new' Labour has come to describe its policy towards school diversity as concerned with the way in which the education system is structured so as to enable schools to differentiate themselves according to their individual ethos, special character and areas of specialist expertise, citing the historical nature of school diversity in Britain as its justification. Thus is history maligned and it is made evident that questions of structure were what Labour said they were – those that did not raise awkward questions about entitlement and equality. Symptomatically, what initially looked like the makings of a distinctive shift towards the reform of urban schools that directed more resources, some again derived from the private sector, to a school or groups of schools serving disadvantaged communities, seemed to appear in programmes, such as EAZs but were soon abandoned. Others, like the ongoing Excellence in Cities programme may last longer and, like Fabian, slowly get there. But the flagship policy since 1997 has been engendering school diversity through variations on the theme of specialist schools, to which we now turn in more detail.

Specialist schools

Figure 8.1 illustrates the year-on-year rise in the number of specialist schools, including their rapid expansion from 1994. In 2003 there were 1,686 specialist schools, which accounted for 54 per cent of all state-funded secondary schools in England. A target exists to have 2,000 specialist schools by 2006.

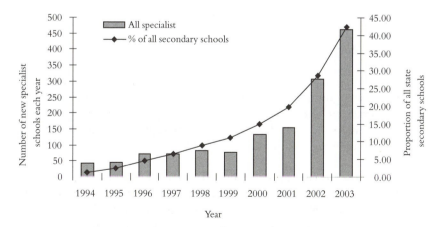

Figure 8.1 The rise of specialist schools, by year: England, 1994–2003 (Source: adapted from Gorard *et al.*, 2003)
Note: figures are given for September of each year.

Specialist schools must continue to deliver the National Curriculum but are meant to provide a special focus on their chosen subject area. Initially specialist school status was only given to GM schools that had a particular strength in technology. But as the number of specialisms was expanded, so too were the types of schools that could apply for specialist status. For many years there were only four specialisms: technology, arts, sports and language. But since 1997 the number of specialisms has risen to ten to include science, business and enterprise, maths, computing, engineering, humanities and music. Schools may now combine them and/or add a 'rural dimension'. Funding was initially capped and application for recognition on a competitive basis. Since the cap was removed in 2002 it has become largely based upon meeting certain requirements including showing that they already have high examination performance or on an upward school improvement trajectory and schools of all types were now allowed to apply, so long as they were not in Special Measures or had serious weaknesses. When applying, schools have to raise £50,000 in unconditional sponsorship towards a capital project. If successful, they can currently expect to receive an additional £100,000 towards it and £126 per pupil per year for four years from the government, in addition to their standard recurrent funding. Specialist schools were expected to spend a third of their additional recurrent funding on sharing their expertise. This might include opening their premises for use by adjacent schools, sharing technology with other schools or enabling staff to lead staff development and share expertise with their teachers. But in light of the competitive environment in which secondary schools found themselves, research suggested that their collaboration tended to be with primary schools or other non-school agencies, rather than other secondaries (Davies *et al.*, 2002; Bell and West, 2003; Penney, 2004). At the same time, the 'exclusive' legacy of the scheme, with some types of schools under- and others over-represented, was declining (Gorard and Taylor, 2001).

Academies

According to the DfES (2004):

> Academies are all-ability schools established by sponsors from business, faith or voluntary groups working in highly innovative partnerships with central government and and local education partners. Sponsors and the Department for Education and Skills (DfES) provide the capital costs for the academy. Running costs are met in full by the DfES.

Sponsors were to be expected to provide up to 20 per cent or £2 million of capital costs and their representatives were expected to join the governing bodies of these schools though, unlike the case of their predecessor CTCs, LEAs were envisaged as key partners in their establishment and development. The first three Academies opened in September 2002, followed by a further nine in 2003. Currently there are 44 open or in development and the government is aiming to have at least 200 in place by 2010, with at least 30 located in London, proving significantly more numerous than CTCs. The rhetoric in establishing Academies has been cast in terms of addressing under-attainment and raising standards. It is the intention, therefore, that they are located in educationally challenging areas and the government stresses that they are all-ability schools. Initially restricted to inner city areas, since the 2002 Education Act they can also be established in challenging suburban and rural areas.

Beacon schools and Leading Edge Partnerships

Beacon schools were identified as high performing and funded to be centres of excellence that shared effective practice and offered advice to other schools. These were established in 1998 and at time of writing numbered 1,052, including 254 secondary, 42 nursery, 678 primary, 6 middle and 71 special schools, each receiving on average an additional £38,000 per year to work with other schools and teachers. Research on these schools to date is limited, although there has been a government-funded review by the NFER (Rudd *et al.*, 2002). Although only operational for six years this scheme is being gradually phased out so that since 2002 secondary Beacon schools have been replaced by the Leading Edge Partnership programme. This adopts a slightly different focus since it tries to identify schools that are already innovative and working in collaboration. Although each has a lead school it is the partnership that receives an additional £60,000 per year for three years. There is no formal 'badging', as in the Beacon school programme, government having accepted that such identification had negative impact and acknowledging the difficulty of getting schools to collaborate when it meant sharing advantage in the market place.

Federations and Diversity Pathfinders

The term 'federation' is used to encompass different types of collaborative groups and/or partnerships and their innovative use heavily promoted by the Institute of Public Policy Research (IPPR), reportedly Labour's most favoured think-tank. The scheme was established in 2001 to demonstrate the 'benefits' of school diversity within particular LEAs. Their definition and objectives are still rather vague though they do entail some formal acknowledgement of collaboration between institutions. The 2002 Education Act allows for federations to have single or joint governing bodies across two or more schools. To date 18 'federations' have been approved. They involve collaborative enterprise led by LEAs that is more about the organisation of school diversity than pedagogic values of collaboration and sharing expertise. There are currently six local authorities in the scheme from urban and rural areas of England, Cornwall, Portsmouth, Newham, Hertfordshire, Birmingham, North Tyneside and two associates. Each is taking a different approach to 'managing' school diversity. For example, in Cornwall the authority is encouraging all maintained secondary schools to obtain specialist school status 'coherently'. In Birmingham, by contrast, six schools are working closely together within a formal management structure, focusing upon staff development, an intranet and building a corporate identity.

Faith-based schools

Although not seen as a formal part of Labour governments' school diversity programme, faith-based schools clearly make a major contribution in offering greater choice of schools and encouraging distinct identities and ethos. New Labour has encouraged their expansion in the wake of *The Way Ahead: Church of England Schools in the New Millennium* (Church Schools Review Group, 2001) and via its own White Paper, *Schools Achieving Success* (DfES, 2001). The former proposed a need for 100 new Church of England secondary schools by 2008 based on excess demand for places, obvious under-provision in some areas and their centrality to its mission and work. The White Paper further argued for the general expansion of faith-based schools, claiming that it was only 'fair' that such provision should extend beyond the dominance of Anglican and Roman Catholic schools, meeting the needs of other minority faiths by increasing, for example, the number of state-funded Muslim and Jewish schools. Moreover, it took the view that such schools generally achieved higher standards and were, consequently, very popular. The relationship between educational attainment and the nature of faith-based school intakes was not regarded as a problem, an issue we will return to later.

The modernisation of comprehensive schools

A programme of school diversity has been represented as part of the processes seeking to change comprehensive schools to meet the needs of changing society and economy. Secretary of State, Estelle Morris (2001: 4) argued that 'specialist schools have had a lot of nonsense written about them. In fact they are modern comprehensives which gain better results when compared with similar schools, which set more challenging goals and which are supported financially to do so'. This view was shared by the Government's senior advisor on specialist schools, Sir Cyril Taylor, who argued that 'specialist schools are intended to strengthen the comprehensive school system, not to threaten it' (2001b: 15). Moving towards all-ability academies and removing the opportunity for new specialist schools to select a proportion of their intakes in the school diversity programme might be taken as within a comprehensive spirit. Attempts to increase the transparency and fairness of admission processes might also be regarded in the same light, as part of an attempt to regain some centralised management and control of school admissions. However, the tentative steps that have been taken entail nothing like returning to control over admissions at levels seen in earlier decades. Although LEAs have been given increased responsibility and some coordination of procedures now exists between schools, most of the changes have taken the form of guidance notes and were heavily influenced by particular tensions that are virtually unique to London. These efforts are characteristic of what Paterson (2003) refers to as

'New Social Democracy', a concern that government should attempt to limit or reconcile the social injustices of the market, that has threaded its way discernibly, if as a minor motif, through Labour's approach to education reforms.

School diversity and social equity

There are two main equity issues that are of importance in terms of school diversity. The first is whether school reforms, whatever form they take, have had an equitable impact on the education standards of all pupils and groups, the second whether changes in school provision has led to greater or lesser segregation of pupils on the basis of their social and ethnic characteristics. Not only does increasing or decreasing segregation of children from different social backgrounds have a direct influence upon the relative performance of schools, as measured by public examination results, it also has an important impact on social mobility, citizenship and social exclusion/inclusion. Equity issues are our first consideration before addressing those of standards.

It is still too soon to identify the overall impact of New Labour's school diversity programme on social equity. Many of its features have only recently been introduced or have already been modified, ensuring something of a research vacuum where relationships between policy and impact have been difficult to define, let alone ascertain, accurately. However, it is possible to examine the longer-term impact of some programmes that pre-date 1997 and recent trends in the socio-economic composition of school intakes. These findings may begin to give some indication of what the consequences of the most recent of reforms might look like.

We have been examining the impact of increased marketisation on socio-economic and ethnic segregation over the last few years (see Gorard *et al.*, 2003) by examining change in the composition of all secondary school intakes in England and Wales, year-on-year, since 1989 and identifying the spatial variation of trends in segregation between schools. As assessed by the proportion of pupils with a specific characteristic who would have to exchange schools for it to be spread evenly, socio-economic segregation of student composition declined from 1988–97. This decline in segregation has been measured in terms of poverty, special needs, first language and ethnicity. The period involved increasing parental choice, a growth in out-of-catchment placements and a large growth in appeals (Taylor, 2001a; Taylor *et al.*, 2002). A number of key factors that may explain these changes relate to: the geography of local education markets, including residential segregation; local school reorganisation and, particularly, the impact of LEAs in closing or amalgamating schools; and the impact of admission procedures. We have already referred to the proliferation of admission processes and practices to emerge from the increased quasi-marketisation of schooling throughout the 1980s and 1990s. Many changes have primarily been a direct consequence of increasing school diversity.

Since 1997 socio-economic segregation in England has begun to rise slightly, for which there are potentially many explanations, particularly at the local level.

Figure 8.2 employs a segregation index, discussed in detail elsewhere (Gorard *et al.*, 2003), to show the spread of children who receive FSM and showing the proportion of FSM children who would have to move school for each school to take its fair share.

About a third of FSM children would have to change school in order to achieve an even spread. If the segregation index were to show 0, all schools would have their fair share of FSM children and, by this criterion, be socio-economically mixed. The higher the index, the more segregated or different in terms of their intakes schools are. A very high segregation index figure would denote a system clearly divided, say, into so-called 'privileged' and 'sink' schools. If the index rises or falls over time schools have become more or less segregated. This figure illustrates that in Wales, where the 'bog standard comprehensive' has been unchallenged by GM, fee-paying, selective or specialist schools, there are markedly lower levels of segregation than the English average. One possible conclusion is that choice without diversity, as referred to here, leads to lower levels of segregation than simple allocation of school places by area of residence (Taylor and Gorard, 2001).

Although levels of segregation in England in 2001 remained lower than they were in 1989 when open enrolment was first introduced, this conceals great variation in levels of segregation in different regions and locales. In general LEAs with higher proportions of foundation, selective or specialist schools have higher levels of socio-economic stratification between schools (Gorard and Fitz, 2000). Within LEAs the relationship between school types and segregation is an ogival one, meaning the relationship between the variables can move in two directions. Areas with high levels of selective, voluntary aided, grant-maintained or fee-

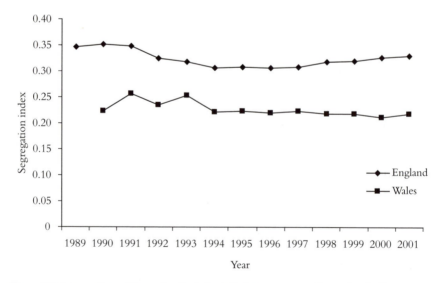

Figure 8.2 Segregation of free school meal pupils between secondary schools (Source: from Gorard *et al.*, 2003: 50)

paying schools had higher levels of segregation than their neighbours and showed no change in segregation over time (e.g. Bromley, Buckinghamshire and Haringey). Areas with large changes in segregation over time or lower initial levels of segregation contained only LEA-controlled comprehensive schools. Diversity with choice, therefore, appears to tend toward segregation/selection. This remains the case in the analysis of our national dataset whatever the criteria of allocation to schools are (and the considerable range of these criteria can be seen in White *et al.*, 2001). These general findings spell out a possible warning for policies, such as the current one that combines parental choice, school diversity and autonomy in allocating school places.

Detailed analysis has also been undertaken of the relationship between socio-economic segregation and specialist schools (Gorard and Taylor, 2001) juxta-posing examination of the changing nature of school intakes including interviews with local authority admissions officers and senior staff from specialist and non-specialist schools. It concluded that it would appear that specialist school programmes *per se* do not lead, as critics have feared, to a two-tier system of admissions. However, specialist schools that retain some autonomy over their admissions arrangements are less likely to admit pupils living in poverty. But combining 'specialist school' with 'school autonomy' diversification (including control over entry), as represented by voluntary aided and foundation schools, was leading to a two-tier education system. This process arises in two stages. First, specialist school status increases the popularity of a school (West *et al.*, 2000), which then must apply some criteria in allocating places when over-subscribed. Second, their oversubscription criteria can then be applied to ensure they recruit more able and more socially 'advantaged' children. Table 8.1 outlines the proportion of schools in England whose intakes have become more 'privileged' over the five years 1994/5–1999/2000. Schools with more 'privileged' intakes already had less than their 'fair share' of children from families in poverty, as measured by their entitlement to FSM and this proportion declined further over the five years. 'Fair shares' were assumed to be the equivalent to the pro-portion of such pupils across all schools in their local authority. Using local authority categories in this way was not only convenient but, more importantly, revealed trends that were very similar to findings derived by using other methods (Taylor *et al.*, 2003). It is important to note that, in such an analysis, the decision being made is a binary one between schools that have become more 'privileged' and those that have not. It does not consider to what extent they have become more 'privileged' (Fitz *et al.*, 2003).

Table 8.1 shows that 29 per cent of all secondary schools and 23 per cent of community schools without any form of diversity had increasingly more 'privileged' intakes over the period. In other words, these schools were allocating relatively fewer places to pupils eligible for free school meals than other schools in their local authority and over time admitted even less. It is these schools, in effect, that have been driving the levels of segregation between schools upwards since 1996–7 (see Figure 8.1). Table 8.1 also illustrates that 37 per cent of specialist schools had more 'privileged' intakes, more than non-specialist schools. It is

Table 8.1 Schools with increasingly more 'privileged' intakes, 1994/5–1999/2000

School type	% schools more 'privileged'
All schools	29
Grammar schools	75
Community schools (no element of diversity)	23
Foundation schools (not grammar)	31
Voluntary aided schools (not grammar)	45
Comprehensive (14–18)	69
Secondary modern	17
Specialist schools (all):	37
Of which language colleges	43
Of which foundation schools	43
Of which voluntary aided schools	57

important to note, however, that 63 per cent of specialist schools did not become more 'privileged'. They may have admitted fewer pupils eligible for FSM but, if they did, then they were already taking more than their 'fair share'. But once we examine in detail different types of specialist schools it becomes clear that particular specialist schools were more likely to become 'privileged' than others. For example, those that chose to specialise in, say, languages were more likely to become 'privileged'. These contrasted, for example, with schools that chose to specialise in sports, which were less likely to become more 'privileged'. Furthermore, as proposed above, a higher proportion of schools with more 'privileged' intakes occurred where schools combined their specialist status with further autonomy and diversity. For example, 43 per cent of specialist foundation and 57 per cent of specialist faith-based, voluntary aided schools increased their 'privileged' intakes over that period.

Table 8.1 also shows that, though few in number, grammar schools that would have for many decades admitted socio-economically privileged intakes prior to open enrolment and greater school diversity, perhaps surprisingly, had become even *more* 'privileged' between 1995–2000. Of course, all of these schools already admitted relatively far fewer pupils eligible for free school meals than the average for their area, meeting the first criterion of already admitting below their 'fair share'. It now also seems highly likely that the fight for places at such schools has increased since open enrolment was introduced. With greater competition for places at grammar schools the benchmark at age 11+ tests will have risen. This, in turn, may have reduced the opportunity for children from relatively poor backgrounds to be allocated a place. Of comprehensive 14–18 schools, many of which were formerly grammar schools prior to the 1970s (Kerckhoff *et al.*, 1996), 69 per cent also became more 'privileged'. In contrast, only 17 per cent of secondary modern schools admitted more 'privileged' intakes during this period.

Table 8.1 also illustrates the elite status of two other types of schools, particularly foundation schools (typically former GM schools) which were more likely to have admitted more 'privileged' intakes than non-diverse types of schools (31 per cent). Although these schools have benefited in the past from additional resources and continue to have some autonomy in their admissions policies, they have not all been able to use this to gain elite status or privileged intakes. The mix of schools that originally became GM (Fitz *et al.*, 1993) meant that they did not become as popular as some other types. While GM status helped to differentiate some of them in the market place from other, LEA maintained schools their overall impact on the education market has, perhaps, been rather limited (Taylor, 2002).

Faith-based, voluntary aided schools, on the other hand, have come to occupy a unique position in the education market (Taylor, 2002; Ball *et al.*, 1995), just under a half maintaining 'privileged' intakes between 1994–5 and 1999–2000 and admitting even more 'privileged' ones. They have retained the right to control their admissions policies in order to provide places for families who are committed to a religious education and to sustain their ethos. Historically they have been associated with selection, interviewing able, well-motivated children, often acting as havens for disaffected parents seeking an alternative to their neighbourhood comprehensives. Critics have argued, with some justification, that interviews conducted with applicant families can become a convenient form of selection by proxy, a process which screens out less desirable students and families (Toynbee, 2001). Recent studies report that both faith-based and voluntary schools were more likely to use interviews and to employ admissions criteria to 'select out' students than LEA community schools (West and Hind, 2003; Couldron, 2003).

Conclusion

Reforms to encourage school diversity first introduced during the 1980s and early 1990s by Conservative administrations continued under Labour, as well as diverging in a number of ways. Labour continued to follow a neo-liberal programme by expanding school diversity well beyond the scope and extent achieved by previous Conservative administrations. By 2004 the specialist schools programme included more than half of all state-funded secondary schools in England and Academies exceeded the number of CTCs introduced by the Conservatives. Labour has also distinctively focused on urban reform, supporting schools in disadvantaged communities, though policies intended to achieve this have not been without controversy based, as they were, on partnerships with private and not-for-profit organisations. There were also questions as to whether diversity, as represented by EAZs and Excellence in Cities, yielded either more resources for schools under stress or better results in public examinations. These programmes represented, in Paterson's terms, attempts to mute the impact of the market on schools vulnerable to it. Labour's determination to close grammar schools, however, was irresolute from the start, giving parents the right to ballot for their closure only on terms that were very difficult to achieve. Nonetheless, the opportunity now exists for grammar schools to become non-selective and local authorities have been given Admission Adjudicators with some power, through admission forums, to reduce the level of academic selection among other schools. While these actions could have been stronger, authorities, such as Hertfordshire, have used these mechanisms to considerably reduce the level of selection among their schools. Selection, however, remains an issue that continues to cause discomfort among Labour's supporters. They might have drawn comfort from the fact that very few specialist schools have chosen to select a proportion of their intakes on aptitude and the embarrassment of successive Ministers in having to defend the practice has now been removed by preventing it in future. Academies, unlike their predecessors, cannot academically select their intakes.

Another key feature of New Labour's approach to school diversity has been the importance placed on school collaboration. Specialist schools, even prior to 1997, were meant to use some of their additional resources to share expertise with neighbouring schools. This flew in the face of the fact that such schools would wish to retain their relative advantage in the education market place. Collaborating, cooperating and/or sharing their expertise and additional resources ran counter to the competitive nature of the established education market. It is perhaps not surprising, therefore, that collaborative links have tended to emerge predominantly with feeder primary schools and not other, non-specialist secondary schools (Yeomans *et al.*, 2000; OFSTED, 2001). The Diversity Pathfinders strategy that helps local authorities, such as Cornwall in encouraging schools to obtain specialist status in a complementary, rather than competitive, way may assuage some of these difficulties. Beacon schools were also introduced to enable collaboration and sharing of expertise and good practice. However, further differentiating some schools and not others in the education market place in this way actually had the potential to severely constrain greater collaboration and prevent the spread of bottom-up innovation in teaching and learning that was envisaged. The secondary sector Leading Edge Partnerships which have replaced them have continued to try and find a way of achieving this ostensibly social democratic objective within its diversity agenda. Instead of identifying schools of excellence and then encouraging them to share their expertise, Leading Edge Partnerships were chosen because they already work effectively in partnership and resources are managed by the partnerships, not individual schools.

Do these elements in Labour's secondary school policies amount to a rediscovery of 'comprehensive principles'? Encouraging greater collaboration between schools might characterise what Paterson (2003) referred to as 'New Social Democracy' except that government would appear to argue that it only represents the modernisation of comprehensive schooling. This might simply be to avoid frightening the horses. However, given that the period of comprehensivisation never really produced homogeneity in schooling (Brighouse, 2002) either through equalised intakes or pedagogic practices, its 'modernisation' appears to be whatever policy makers decree. If Ministers and policy advisors are claiming an effective return to the pursuit of social equity, for many a desirable aim of comprehensive schooling, then they may also be mistaken. We have provided clear evidence that, after 1997, socio-economic segregation between all secondary schools in England has continued to rise and Labour's education agenda has, at least as yet, made no difference in this respect. We have also demonstrated that, for example, in Wales, where school diversity is limited, socioeconomic segregation between secondary schools is significantly lower than in England and continued to decline when segregation in England began to rise. However, we are talking about countries where not only secondary school structures but class distributions are different. We have to recognise, at the same time, that, notwithstanding what Ministers sometimes promise that they are capable of and school improvement gurus hold forth as examplars, in these respects schools are not capable of being 'turned round' like high powered light craft but behave more like heavily laden tankers.

Some schools who controlled their own admissions policies admitted increasingly 'privileged' intakes from 1994–5 to 1999–2000 and, under the rules that have operated in England, it would seem that pursuing a programme of school diversity leads to greater social inequity. To obtain specialist school status under the criteria of most schemes that have operated, pupils must already have been achieving high examination standards or show that they were already improving. A combination of additional resources, growing popularity and autonomy over admissions has allowed some schools, whether consciously or not, to recruit more able children and from more advantaged socio-economic backgrounds. Attracting more able pupils is more than likely to result in improvement of their overall examination performance. Such evidence of increasing education standards has been used by governments to further encourage school diversity. Yet it ought to come as no surprise that, with additional resources and growing popularity, specialist schools programmes appear successful. But the game is fixed and similar concerns must exist about the evidence base for further expansion of faith-based schooling. Moreover, expansion in the number of city academies needs to be viewed in the light of these considerations.

Differences in *modus operandi* of school diversity programmes between recent Labour and preceding Conservative governments have lain in the latter primarily seeing it as a way of extending choice within the education market place, bypassing what they believed were largely bureaucratic and inertial local authorities. The former saw it as a vehicle for raising standards in schools which typically have been offered additional resources in return for reforming their teaching and learning, organisation and/or governance in 'desired' ways. The problem with this is that the 'other' community schools that remain with no formal, special 'status' are not offered additional resources. Inevitably, this leads to growing disparity between 'winners' and 'losers'. It is difficult to see how encouraging greater collaboration between schools can overcome such disparity. Fostering greater cooperation and networking between schools as a strategy to raise standards across all of them naively ignores the presence of school choice and competition that are now a firm system feature in England. If governments wish to 'modernise' comprehensive schooling for a changing society they must first recognise that the rules governing the system's control, shape and rationales for the production and consumption of education have changed considerably since the 1970s.

Acknowledgement

This chapter draws on an unpublished paper originally presented at the AERA Annual Meeting in New Orleans in 2002. The authors wish to acknowledge the contribution of Stephen Gorard and Chris Taylor for generating the tables and figures used.

9   Further reading

Both the joy and the pain of getting to grips with policy studies is its many-sidedness as a knowledge 'region'. Even when we delimit our view to sociological approaches and education, we face the prospect of grappling with a complex aspect of social life using a discipline that is itself weakly horizontally structured. We offer here some suggestions for reading around and more deeply into a range of issues, based as much on what we know has helped our students as judgements of what has 'moved the field'. Getting the events of the past sixty years into perspective is undoubtedly helped, in our view, by having a working grasp of antecedent nineteenth- and early twentieth-century events in the education system. Among those that are highly readable and accessible, we would place Sanderson (1985, 1994), Aldrich (1996), Jones (1997) and Jones (2003). Also, Mackinnon et al. (1996) provide a most useful summary of reports, legislation and the overall shape of the education system. For those who need a general textbook on modern Britain within which to context education, Abercrombie and Warde (2000, 2001) may suit.

A knowledge of the 'machinery of government', the working parts of the ORF, of how Ministers, legislative processes and quangos produce, scrutinise and begin to put into effect authoritative decisions is greatly demystifying and can be approached through Budge et al. (2004) and Rhodes (1997), while the admirable series edited by Dunleavy and others, currently in its seventh volume (2003), details change over most of the past two decades. On the wider context of the changing relation of central to local government and the rise of the quango state, Sharpe's (1993) own contributions to his edited volume are valuable. It is difficult to find a source that deals head on with the range of agencies that impinge upon government, attempting to secure their ends by influencing its legislative and administrative behaviour in education, very often as part of their wider activities as pedagogic recontextualising agencies.

Among the number of books that set out to offer general reviews of educational policy, Trowler (1998, 2003) offer some sense of the latter and a good deal more. Including helpful summaries of landmarks in term of educational policy events, particularly since 1979 and overviews of theories and processes of policy making. Taylor et al. (1997) paint a rich series of pictures of how such relationships seek to work, mainly in an Australian context but relating them strongly to wider issues of globalisation and class, gender and ethnic struggle for change. Coffey (2000) argues for a more sociological approach to educational policy analysis, focusing more on its effect than processes in Britain. Levin (2001) looks at the effects of New Right policies across five countries, attempting to balance structure and contingency and generally coming down on the side of the latter.

Having grasped some of the issues concerned with the changing nature of the state in relation to various aspects of economic, social and cultural processes, in which Jordan (1985) is also very helpful, Western Welfare States can be seen to have developed both in uniform and different – 'exceptional' – ways. Their historical core had much to do with providing degrees of social security for old age, unemployment, widowhood and health. Skocpol's (1992) comparatively informed historical case study of the development of American social provision argues that politics create policies and policies remake politics – the best indication of what policy is likely to be is what it was last time. Steinmo and Rothstein (2002) exemplify the institutionalist approach, of which Skocpol's work is an exemplar, while Taylor-Gooby (1991) looks at the failure of the grand tradition of the welfare state and the case for its retention. Twine (1994) relates the complex structures of taxation to differing types of welfare state regimes. In areas outside of education analyses, such as Saunders (1996) initially developed with respect of urban and housing issues (1981) and Wall and Owen (1999) with respect to the Health Service, there are many parallels and insights for questions of educational provision. Schools, like taxes, are even older than welfare states but only come within the ambit of public finance when need for their mass provision outgrew private, mainly religious, means in secularising nineteenth-century societies, since when programme and funding crises have been endemic. Glennerster (1992) presents the public finance issues with clarity while Thomas (1990) exemplifies cost-effectiveness issues that policy makers constantly weigh against other considerations.

Most sociological studies of educational policy make reference to its relation to social change. Cahill (1994) sees old inequalities in the context of the new as traditional categories, such as education, housing and social security have to be recast in the context of communicating, viewing, travelling, shopping, working and playing. Much of the terms of the debate about the forces and relations underlying such change have been analysed in terms of the passing from Fordism to post-Fordism, as revealed in Burrows and Loader (1994). This material may be read usefully alongside Clarke *et al.* (1994), Clark *et al.* (2000) and Cutler and Waine (1994, 1997). Analyses of the wholesale importation of private sector management ideas and techniques into the public sector, sometimes referred to as new public management, associated with the transition, involving devolved budgets, business and development plans, performance indicators and target setting have become the watchword in education, health and other areas.

Ahier and Flude (1983) justly referred to the re-emergence in the sociology of education of questions of political rather than mainly neo-marxist economic determination of educational policy. Certainly Kogan's work from 1975 represented an attempt to shift from pluralist and procedural versions of policy and change to include considerations of power and ideology in a social meliorist tradition of politics and education still represented in, for example, Halpin *et al.* (2004). Tapper and Salter's work (Tapper and Salter, 1978; Salter and Tapper, 1981) also put theoretical considerations into areas formerly dominated by mere description. By the end of the 1980s, Edwards *et al.* (1989) had completed their work on the assisted-places scheme and Dale (1989) and Gleeson (1989) on TVEI. These studies and others (for example, Fitz *et al.*, 1993; Whitty *et al.*, 1996; Power *et al.*, 2003) that followed, investigating policy origins, destinations and impact, exemplified the so-called 'policy turn' in the sociology of education where, no longer seeing any opportunity to influence policy through funded research undertaken on their own initiative, sociologists turned their skills and orientation to the analysis of policy making and policy implementation in the study of grant-maintained schools, CTCs, EAZs and private education.

The 1988 Act released a small flood of commentary and reportage, the best known of the latter being Maclure (1989) and among the more stimulating, Knight (1990). It also intensified the debate about and research into the purported impact of choice and competition policies on schools and schooling. Its epicentre has always been the USA and, for a full-frontal explication of the supposed benefits of organizing education on market principles, Chubb and Moe's (1990) *Politics, Markets and America's Schools*, sets out a case against the 'one best system' of common schooling. In the UK, Tooley's (2000) *Reclaiming Education* sets out the case for unbounded choice and competition policies in British education. Given the success of the per capita funding regime as it now applies to British schools and its capacity to provide more money to schools that are recruiting well and reduce support for those which do not, the 'voucher debate' has cooled in the UK. In the USA, however, it has maintained a significant place on the policy agenda. Witte's (1990) study of the Milwaukee voucher programme takes a cool look at a targeted programme by a scholar who has considerable sympathy for vouchers.

The best known name in the field in Britain from the 1990s has been Ball (1990, 1994, 2003) who, with others, has undertaken research in school choice, markets and class relations in education that have drawn successively, among others, upon interactionism, Foucault, Bourdieu and Bernstein. Along with Burgess and Goodson he has run the *Journal of Educational Policy* for 20 years. Gewirtz *et al.* (1995) set the tone for British research on 'school choice' in two ways: by reporting that education markets increased the social stratification of schools and by employing a design based on small scale, field-work intensive, qualitative research. This strategy was also adopted in an influential New Zealand study (Lauder *et al.*, 1999) that came to broadly similar conclusions. The market impact wars really broke out when Gorard *et al.* (2003) drew on data from all 24,000 schools in England and Wales over a 13-year period and reported that markets had much less impact on the stratification of schools than was claimed by market advocates and its critics.

The whole emphasis upon funded research in education generally has swung in the last decade or so to a 'programme' basis where policy makers themselves specify and prioritise broad areas within which projects are invited to compete for resources, such as *The Learning Society* (Coffield, 2000) and *Teaching and Learning* (www.tlrp.org). In the latter, teams were given the brief to explore 'what works' and the way the programme was established was itself an explicit critique of both the quality and direction of British educational research which was thought, unlike medical research, to offer not much help or guidance to professionals going about their daily business.

One of the best ways to begin further reading of Bernstein's own work is through the prefaces or introductory essays that he wrote to each of his books (1971, 1973, 1975, 1990, 1996. All of these, apart from the 1973 *Volume II* on language, also have revised editions). These introductions are partly auto-biographic but mainly concerned to show how his ideas revealed continuity and development. In a vital sense, *Volume V* in 1996 synthesised and ordered the earlier work and Chapter 1 in this book refers to it mainly. His 1999 paper on horizontal and vertical discourse, the short piece that he wrote just a few months before his death in 2000 for a conference on his work in Lisbon and the rather poignant transcript of his video link conversation recorded at it (Bernstein, 2001a, 2001b) are also important from our argument's point of view. While Atkinson (1985) analysed Bernstein's earlier sociolinguistic and educational work with admirable clarity no one has yet attempted to put the remainder to detailed analysis, let alone the whole. However, there have been two *festschriften* (Atkinson *et al.*, 1995; Sadovnik, 1995) and two books based on work presented at conferences at Lisbon and Cape Town (Morais *et al.*, 2001; Muller *et al.*, 2004) which contain strong selections of the most up-to-date research work based on his ideas. A number of their papers have already been referred to in various chapters above and more are indicated below. Arnot *et al.* (2002) devoted a deliberately expository volume of the *British Journal of Sociology of Education* to his work, in which Parlo Singh's contribution is of particular value.

In plugging the several gaps in our work, in the area of primary education we would point to the remarkable compilation in Alexander (2001) on contrasting systems and his gripping account (1997) of some of the machinations behind policy formation in which he became somewhat involved and Galton (1998, 1999) who reviews work, with several others, of the ORACLE project and after. None are deeply sociological but all provide grist to the mill in thinking through pedagogic discourse. Dyson and Slee (2001) specifically address how policy focus on standards and social inclusion impinges on special education. On further education, Ainley and Bailey (1997) anatomise the 1990s while Jephcote and Huddleston (2001) offer a briefer comment. Rees and Stroud (2001) provide a good overview of policy issues in higher education, while on wider issues of the relation of education and training to labour markets, Ashton and Green (1996) has been pivotal, Ahier and Esland (1999) is highly accessible, Gorard and Rees (2002) report on one of the more pointed *Learning Society* projects and Hodgson and Spours (1999) are concerned with British 14+ training agendas. Maton (2004) offers a Bernsteinian analysis of the new universities, seeking to add the notion of epistemic to the pedagogic device. The choice available on gender and education policy is now rich. Delamont (1996, 2001) provides historical and theoretical settings, Holland (1997) reviews the issues succinctly, while Arnot *et al.* (1996, 1999) and Salisbury and Riddell (1999) focus on policy and change. On ethnicity and race, Fuller (1997) is a splendid brief introduction, while Gillborn and Youdell (1999) show particularly how 'market' policies work adversely on minority student fates and Wright *et al.* (2000) (as others do) how 'race', class and gender interact to produce disadvantages. Among recent texts that have set out to deal explicitly with class, gender and race issues in relation to postwar policy, Tomlinson (2001) is wonderfully clear. The collection edited by Phillips and Furlong (2001) not only has valuable contributions to make to these same issues but also on special needs, inclusion and 'ages and stages' from primary to further and higher education, as well as teacher education.

While questions of opportunity and educability raised by survey studies in the 1950s and 1960s led to a number of contrasting single school-based investigations, including Cicourel and Kitsuse (1963) in suburban USA, Dale and Griffith (1965) in Swansea, and Hargreaves (1967) and Lacey (1970) in Manchester, all centrally concerned with mainly social class assortative power of 'streams' and 'tracks' (a genre that ran on to Ball, 1981 and Evans, 1985), none of these earlier studies reported classroom experience systematically, though it was clear that researchers had spent considerable time there. Even when studies like Brandis and Young (1967) and Banks and Finlayson (1973) insinuated differently, what happened in secondary classrooms remained obscure. The strongly contrasting theoretical styles of studies, such as Rist (1970), Nash (1973), Delamont (1976) and Sharp and Green (1975), focussed mainly on primary school contexts, initiated two decades of classroom studies that remained mainly quite fixated on class, gender, ethnic and (dis)ability effects of teaching and learning processes. These were, in turn, explicated largely with reference to teacher expectations and labelling processes, then teaching style, in ways that completely justified Bernstein's observations that sociologists were obsessed with education's 'relations to' these categories than to the neglect of its 'relations within'; pedagogy really appeared to have no voice of its own (Davies, 1981, 1994, 1995). Task perspective approaches producing studies focussing on 'match' and 'opportunity to learn' have led to attempts, such as Pollard's (1990) to move toward the latter. Among Bernstein's own students, Morais (formerly Domingos), has, with her associates now developed techniques for anatomising, operation-alising and manipulating pedagogic practices through in-service research and development work with Portugese teachers. Through them they have evolved and tested 'mixed pedagogies' involving manipulation of teachers' instructional and regulative practices and students' recognition of their abilities to realise their requirements. These are shown to produce remarkable increments in working-class students' achievement in school science, both absolutely and relative to their middle-class counterparts, including areas of high cognitive demand. This work can be initially accessed through Morais *et al.* (2004) and Neves *et al.* (2004). In England, Daniels (1989) initially also studied pupil's recognition and realisation rules in relation to discursive, organisational and interactive practices in special education. Some of their more recent work (Daniels *et al.*, 2004), combining Bernsteinian and Vygotskyan perspectives, has focused on the gendering of learner identity. Arnot and Reay (2004) consider the effects of contrasting modalities of instructional and pedagogic discourse on class and gender identities in two English secondary schools and several other papers in the same volume, as in Morais *et al.* (2001), deal with similar themes.

Throughout this volume we have also drawn attention to both the shortcomings and exemplary features of the 'political arithmetic' tradition in educational policy analysis and in the field of the sociology of education. The male focus and lack of detail on ethnic mobility patterns in the early mobility studies has been widely recognised and scholars in the social mobility field will admit that too much of their energy has been drawn into technical battles over fine points of design and statistical elegance. But in recent decades, social mobility studies have become almost invisible in educational studies and in the sociology of education. While the most cited study in this area would have been Halsey *et al.* (1980), other powerful studies go uncited. Including, most astonishingly, Marshall *et al.* (1997), *Against All Odds*. Some of the best educational research is being done outside university departments of education by them and others like Prandy and his colleagues (2003, 2004), Blackburn and Marsh (1991), Goldthorpe (2003) and scholars at the LSE's Centre for Economic Performance (CEP), Blanden, Machin and Vignoles (now at the Institute of Education, University of London) and Galindo-Rueda who continue to work the data contained in the two British cohort studies alongside the most recent employment data sets. CEP papers and reports can be downloaded from http://cep.lse.ac.uk/pubs.

Education is not bereft of scholars whose work is cognate with that of the social mobility theorists although they are few in number. Paterson (2001) continues the strong Edinburgh tradition of investigating longitudinally patterns of inequality and education in Britain. Bynner and his colleagues (Bynner and Joshi, 2002) at the Institute of Education, University of London's Centre for Longitudinal Studies (see also www.cls.ioe.ac) are doing work that now takes on a new importance in the Millennium Cohort Study, intended to complement the 1958 and 1970 surveys. In addition all school children in England and Wales have been assigned, or are about to have, a 'unique pupil identifier' so that an individual's progress can be followed throughout their school career. It also provides an important opportunity to correct the biases of earlier cohort studies.

For academics, educational professionals and policy makers seriously interested in 'evidence-based policy making', the social mobility studies are good places to begin, if only because it clearly delimits what education polices can and cannot do. For anyone in need of measured accounts of the impact of major educational policy changes on the structure of opportunity or changes in the life chances and employment prospects of children from different classes, a dip into social mobility studies is a much needed antidote to the claims of government optimists and their boosters, school management gurus, school effectiveness transformers and sundry educational entrepreneurs. When it comes to the big stuff, like closing attainment gaps, enhancing staying on rates or opening up employment opportunities for students in Ebbw Vale or Sunderland, having read and marked the social mobility literature, in the spirit of Monty Python, we should ask, 'What did the National College of School Leadership and its mojo ever do for you'?

Gorard is another person in education who has made an important contribution to our understanding of the persistence in the patterns of education and inequality over spans of time. His influence pervades much of this book. *Education and Social Justice* (Gorard, 2000) exemplifies the very best of his work that brings together hard facts about the outcomes of schools in Wales and England alongside a clear explication of how to apply the techniques of political arithmetic to educational policy analysis. His exegesis of the 'politicians error', the misreading and misinterpretation and reporting of percentage increases or decreases in outputs, and his advocacy of proportionate methods of analysis shows how revealing secondary analysis of official data can be achieved via simple arithmetic techniques; a calculator, pen and paper. There may be hope for us all.

Bibliography

Abercrombie, N. and Warde, A. (2000) *Contemporary British Society*, Cambridge: Polity Press.

Abercrombie, N. and Warde, A. (2001) *Contemporary British Society Reader*, Cambridge: Polity Press.

Ahier, J. and Esland, G. (eds) (1999) *Education, Training and the Future of Work. 1, Social, Political and Economic Contexts of Policy Development*, London: Routledge, in association with the Open University.

Ahier, J. and Flude, M. (eds) (1983) *Contemporary Education Policy*, London: Croom Helm.

Ainley, P. and Bailey, B. (1997) *The Business of Learning*, London: Cassell.

Aldrich, R. (1996) *Education for the Nation*, London: Cassell.

Aldridge, S. (2001) *Social Mobility: A Discussion Paper*, London: Performance and Innovation Unit.

Alexander, R.J. (1996) *Other Primary Schools and Ours: Hazards of International Comparison*, Warwick: Centre for Research in Elementary and Primary Education.

Alexander, R.J. (1997) *Policy and Practice in Primary Education: Local Initiative, National Agenda*, London: Routledge.

Alexander, R.J. (2001) *Culture and Pedagogy: International Comparisons in Primary Education*, Oxford: Blackwell.

Al-Ramahi, N. and Davies, B. (2002) 'Changing primary education in Palestine: pulling in several directions at once', *International Studies in Sociology of Education*, 12(1): 59–76.

Arnot, M. and Reay, D. (2004) 'The framing of pedagogic encounters: regulating the social order in classroom learning', in J. Muller, B. Davies and A. Morais (eds) *Reading Bernstein, Researching Bernstein*, London: RoutledgeFalmer.

Arnot, M., David, M. and Weiner, G. (1996) *Educational Reforms and Gender Equality in Schools*, Manchester: Equal Opportunities Commission.

Arnot, M., David, M. and Weiner, G. (1999) *Closing the Gender Gap: Postwar Education and Social Change*, Cambridge: Polity Press.

Arnot, M. *et al.* (2002) 'Basil Bernstein's theory of social class, educational codes and social control', *British Journal of Sociology of Education*, 23(4): Special Issue.

Ashton, D.N. and Green, F. (1996) *Education, Training and the Global Economy*, Cheltenham: Edward Elgar.

Atkinson, P. (1985) *Language, Structure and Reproduction: The Sociology of Basil Bernstein*, London: Methuen.

Atkinson, P., Davies, B. and Delamont, S. (eds) (1995) *Discourse and Reproduction. Essays in Honour of Basil Bernstein*, Cresskill, NJ: Hampton Press.

Ball, S.J. (1981) *Beachside Comprehensive: A Case Study of Secondary Schooling*, Cambridge: Cambridge University Press.

Ball, S.J. (1990) *Politics and Policymaking in Education*, London: Routledge.

Ball, S.J. (1994) *Education Reform: A Critical and Post-structural Approach*, Buckingham: Open University Press.

Ball, S.J. (1998) 'Big policies/small world: an introduction to international perspectives in educational policy', *Comparative Education*, 34(2): 119–30.

Ball, S.J. (2000) 'Performativities and fabrications in the education economy: towards the performative society', *Australian Educational Researcher*, 27(2): 1–24.

Ball, S.J. (2003) *Class Strategies and the Education Market: The Middle Classes and Social Advantage*, London: RoutledgeFalmer.

Ball, S.J., Bowe, R. and Gewirtz, S. (1995) 'Circuits of schooling: a sociological explanation of parental choice in social class contexts', *Sociological Review*, 43(1): 52–87.

Banks, O. (1955) *Parity And Prestige In English Secondary Education: A Study in Educational Sociology*, London: Routledge.

Banks, O. and Finlayson, D. (1973) *Success and Failure in the Secondary School*, London: Methuen.

Barker-Lunn, J. and Ferri, E. (1970) *Streaming in the Primary School*, Slough: National Foundation for Educational Research (NFER).

Bell, D. (1960) *The End of Ideology: The Exhaustion of the Political Ideas of the Fifties*, Glencoe, IL: Free Press.

Bell, D. (1973) *Coming of Post-Industrial Society: A Venture in Social Forecasting*, New York: Basic books.

Bell, D. and Richie, R. (1999) *Towards Effective Subject Leadership in the Primary School*, Buckingham: Open University Press.

Bell, K. and West, A. (2003) 'Specialist schools: an exploration of competition and co-operation', *Educational Studies*, 29(2–3): 273–89.

Bellaby, P. (1977) *The Sociology of Comprehensive Schooling*, London: Methuen.

Benn, C. and Chitty, C. (1996) *Thirty Years On: Is Comprehensive Schooling Alive and Well or Struggling to Survive?*, London: David Fulton.

Benn, C. and Simon, B.N. (1982) *Half Way There: Report on British Comprehensive School Reform*, Harmondsworth: Penguin.

Berg, L. (1968) *Risinghill: Death of a Comprehensive*, Harmondsworth: Penguin.

Bernstein, B. (1970) 'Education cannot compensate for society', *New Society*, 377: 344–7.

Bernstein, B. (1971) *Class, Codes and Control. Volume 1, Theoretical Studies Towards a Sociology of Language*, London: Routledge and Kegan Paul.

Bernstein, B. (1973) *Class, Codes and Control. Volume 2, Applied Studies Towards a Sociology of Language*, London: Routledge and Kegan Paul.

Bernstein, B. (1975) *Class, Codes and Control. Volume 3, Towards a Theory of Educational Transmissions*, London: Routledge and Kegan Paul.

Bernstein, B. (1977) 'Aspects of the relation between education and production', in *Class, Codes and Control. Volume 3, Towards a Theory of Educational Transmissions*, 2nd rev. edn, London: Routledge.

Bernstein, B. (1990) *Class, Codes and Control. Volume 4, The Structuring of Pedagogic Discourse*, London: Routledge.

Bernstein, B. (1996) *Pedagogy, Symbolic Control and Identity: Theory, Research, Critique*, London: Taylor & Francis.

Bernstein, B. (1999) 'Vertical and horizontal discourse: an essay', *British Journal of Sociology of Education*, 20(2): 157–73.

Bernstein, B. (2000) *Pedagogy, Symbolic Control and Identity: Theory, Research, Critique*, rev. edn, Oxford: Rowman and Littlefield.

Bernstein, B. (2001a) 'From pedagogies to knowledges', in A. Morais, I. Neves, B. Davies and H. Daniels (eds) *Towards a Sociology of Pedagogy: The Contribution of Basil Bernstein to Research*, New York: Peter Lang.

Bernstein, B. (2001b) 'Video conference with Basil Bernstein', in A. Morais, I. Neves, B. Davies and H. Daniels (eds) *Towards a Sociology of Pedagogy: The Contribution of Basil Bernstein to Research*, New York: Peter Lang.

Blackburn, R.M. and Marsh, C. (1991) 'Education and social class: revisiting the 1944 Education Act with fixed marginals', *British Journal of Sociology*, 42(4): 507–36.

Blanden, J., Gregg, P., Goodman, A. and Machin, S. (2002) *Changes in Intergenerational Mobility in Britain*, London: Centre for Performance, London School of Economics.

Blatchford, P., Bassett, P., Goldstein, H. and Martin, C. (2003) 'Are class size differences related to pupils' educational progress and classroom processes? Findings from the Institute of Education class size study of children aged 5–7 years', *British Educational Research Journal*, 29(5): 709–30.

Boaler, J. (1997) *Experiencing School Mathematics: Teaching Styles and Setting*, Buckingham: Open University Press.

Bowe, R. and Ball, S.J. with Gold, A. (1992) *Reforming Education and Changing Schools: Case Studies in Policy*, London: Routledge.

Bradford, M. (1995) 'Diversification and division in the English education system: towards a post-Fordist model?', *Environment and Planning A*, 27: 1595–612.

Brandis, W. and Young, D. (1967) 'Two types of streaming and their probable application in comprehensive schools', *ULIE Bulletin*, (N.S.) August.

Brighouse, T. (2002) 'Comprehensive schools then, now and in the future: is it time to draw a line on the sand and create a new ideal?', *The Caroline Benn, Brian Simon Memorial Lecture*, September 2002, downloaded from www.socialisteducation.org.uk/benn02.

Brown, M. and Rutherford, D. (1998) 'A re-appraisal of the role of the head of department in UK secondary schools', *Journal of Educational Administration*, 37(3): 229–42.

Brown, P. and Hesketh, A. (2004) *The Mismanagement of Talent: Employability and Jobs in the Knowledge Economy*, Oxford: Oxford University Press.

Budge, I., Crewe, I., McKay, D. and Newton, D. (2004) *The New British Politics*, 3rd edn, London: Pearson Longman.

Burrows, R. and Loader, B. (eds) (1994) *Towards a Post-Fordist Welfare State*, London: Routledge.

Bynner, J. and Joshi, H. (2002) 'Equality and opportunity in education: evidence from the 1958 and 1970 birth cohort studies', *Oxford Review of Education*, 28(2): 405–21.

Byrne, E.M. (1978) *Women in Education*, London: Tavistock.

Cahill, M. (1994) *The New Social Policy*, Oxford: Blackwell.

Campbell, F. (1956) 'Eleven-plus and all that', in H. Silver (1973) *Equal Opportunity in Education*, London: Methuen.

Carvel, J. (1997) 'Shephard tightens test for trainee teachers', *The Guardian*, 15 February: 4.

Castells, M. (1996) *The Rise of the Network Society*, Oxford: Blackwell.

Castells, M. (1997) *The Power of Identity*, Oxford: Blackwell.

Castells, M. (1998) *End of Millennium*, Oxford: Blackwell.

Central Advisory Council for Education (CACE) (England) (1959) *15 to 18, The Crowther Report, Volumes 1 and 2*, London: HMSO.

Central Advisory Council for Education (CACE) (1963) *Half our Future*, London: HMSO.

Central Advisory Council for Education (CACE) (England) (1977) *Children and their Primary Schools, Volumes 1 and 2*, London: HMSO.

Chubb, J and Moe, T. (1990) *Politics, Markets and America's Schools*, Washington, DC: Brookings Institution.

Church Schools Review Group (2001) *The Way Ahead: Church of England Schools in the New Millennium*, London: Church House Publishing.

Cicourel, A.V. and Kitsuse, J. (1963) *The Educational Decision Makers*, Indianapolis, IN: Bobbs-Merrill.

Clarke, C. (2003) *A New Specialist System: Transforming Secondary Education*, London: DfES

Clarke, J., Cochrane, A. and McLaughlin, E. (eds) (1994) *Managing Social Policy*, London: Sage.

Clarke, J., Gewirtz, S. and McLaughlin, E. (eds) (2000) *New Managerialism, New Welfare*, London: Sage.

Coffey, A. (2001) *Education and Social Change*, Buckingham: Open University Press.

Coffield, F. (ed) (2000) *Differing Visions of a Learning Society, Volumes 1 and 2*, Bristol: Policy Press.

Commission for Racial Equality (CRE) (1983) *Secondary School Allocations in Reading*, London: Comission for Racial Equality.

Committee of Enquiry into Reading and the Use of English (1975) *A Language for Life*, London: HMSO.

Committee on Higher Education (1963) *Higher Education (1), Robbins Report*, London: HMSO.

Corbishley, P. (1977) 'Research findings on teaching groups in secondary schools', in B. Davies and R.G. Cave (eds) *Mixed Ability in the Secondary School*, London: Ward Lock.

Couldron, J. (2003) 'Memorandum of evidence presented to the House of Commons Education and Skills Select Committee', *Secondary Education: School Admissions*, London: The Stationery Office.

Cox, C.B. (1981) *Education: The Next Decade*, London: Conservative Political Centre.

Cox, C.B. and Dyson, A.E. (eds) (1969) *Fight for Education: A Black Paper*, London: The Critical Quarterly Society.

Croll, P. (ed) (1996) *Teachers, Pupils and Primary Schooling*, London: Cassell Education.

Cutler, T. and Waine, B. (1994) *Managing the Welfare State: The Politics of Public Sector Management*, Oxford and Providence, RI: Berg.

Cutler, T. and Waine, B. (eds) (1997) *Managing the Welfare State: Text and Sourcebook*, Oxford: Berg.

Dale, R. (1989) *The State and Education Policy*, Buckingham: Open University Press.

Dale, R.R. and Griffith, S. (1965) *Down Stream: Failure in the Grammar School*, London: Routledge and Kegan Paul.

Daniels, H. (1989) 'Visual displays as tacit relays of the structure of pedagogic practice', *British Journal of Sociology of Education*, 10(2): 123–40.

Daniels, H. and Creese, A. with Hey, V. and Leonard, D. (2004) 'Gendered learning identity in two modalities of pedagogic discourse', in J. Muller, B. Davies and A. Morais (eds) *Reading Bernstein, Researching Bernstein*, London: RoutledgeFalmer.

Davies, B. (1973) 'On the contribution of organisational analysis to the study of educational institutions', in R. Brown (ed.) *Knowledge, Education and Cultural Change: Papers in the Sociology of Education*, London: Tavistock.

Davies, B. (1976) *Social Control in Education*, London: Methuen.

Davies, B. (1977) 'Meanings and motives in going mixed ability', in B. Davies and G.G. Cave (eds) *Mixed Ability in the Secondary School*, London: Ward Lock.

Davies, B. (1981) 'The state of schooling', *Educational Analysis*, 3(1): 1–23.

Davies, B. (1994) 'Durkheim and the sociology of education in Britain', *British Journal of the Sociology of Education*, 15(1): 3–25.

Davies, B. (1994) 'On the neglect of pedagogy in educational studies and its consequences', *British Journal of In-service Education*, 20(1): 17–34.

Davies, B. (1995) 'Bernstein on classrooms', in P. Atkinson, B. Davies and S. Delamont (eds) *Discourse and Reproduction*, Cresskill, NJ: Hampton Press.

Davies, B. and Evans, J. (2001) 'Changing cultures and schools in England and Wales', in J. Cairns, D. Lawton and R. Gardner (eds) *Values, Culture and Education, World Yearbook of Education 2001*, London: Kogan Page.

Davies, P., Adnett, N. and Mangan, J. (2002) 'The diversity and dynamics of competition: evidence from two local schooling markets', *Oxford Review of Education*, 28(1): 91–107.

Delamont, S. (1976) *Interaction in the Classroom*, London: Methuen.

Delamont, S. (1996) *A Woman's Place in Education: Historical and Sociological Perspectives on Gender and Education*, Aldershot: Avebury.

Delamont, S. (2001) *Changing Women, Unchanging Men?: Sociological Perspectives on Gender in a Post-industrial Society*, Buckingham: Open University Press.

DFE (1992) *Choice and Diversity: A New Framework for Schools*, London: HMSO.

DfEE (1997) *Excellence in Schools*, London: The Stationery Office.

Department for Education and Skills (DfES) (2001) *Schools Achieving Success*, London: The Stationery Office.

Department for Education and Skills (DfES) (2003) *14–19: Opportunity and Excellence*, London: Department for Education and Skills.

Department for Education and Skills (DfES) (2003b) *A New Specialist System: Transforming Secondary Education*, downloaded from http://teachernet.gov.uk/makingadiff/doct.

Department for Education and Skills (DfES) (2004) 'What are academies? Schools to make a difference', *The Standards Site*, downloaded from http://www.standards.dfes.gov.uk/academies.

Department of Education and Science (DES) (1978) *Comprehensive Education*, London: HMSO.

Dolowitz, D.P., Hulme, R., Nellis, M. and O'Neil, F. (2000) *Policy Transfer and British Social Policy*, Buckingham: Open University Press.

Douglas, J.W.B., Ross, J.M. and Simpson, H.R. (1968) *All Our Futures: A Longitudinal Study of Secondary Schools*, London: Peter Davies.

Doward, J. (2004) 'Class size crisis looms as more teachers quit', *EducationGuardian*, Sunday, 19 December, downloaded from http://www.education.guardian.co.uk/teachershortage/.

Dunleavy, P. (ed.) (2003) *Developments in British Politics*, 7, Basingstoke: Palgrave Macmillan.

Durkheim, E. (1961) *Moral Education: A Study in the Application of the Sociology of Education*, New York: Free Press of Glencoe.

Dyson, A. and Slee, R. (2001) 'Special needs education from Warnock to Salamanca: the triumph of liberalism?', in R. Phillips and J. Furlong (eds) *Education, Reform and the State: Twenty-five years of Politics, Policy and Practice*, London: RoutledgeFalmer.

Earl, L., Watson, N., Levin. B., Leithwood, K. and Fullan, M. (2003) *Watching and Learning 3: The Final Report of the External Evaluation of England's National Literacy and Numeracy Strategies*, Nottingham: DfES.

Education and Skills Committee, House of Commons (2004) *Secondary Education: School Admissions*, 2 vols, London: The Stationery Office.

Edwards, A., Fitz, J. and Whitty, G. (1989) *The State and Private Education: An Evaluation of the Assisted Places Scheme*, Lewes: Falmer.

Erikson, R. and Goldthorpe, J. (1992) *The Constant Flux: A Study of Class Mobility in Industrial Societies*, Oxford: Oxford University Press.

Esland, G. (1996) 'Education, training and nation-state capitalism: Britain's failing strategy', in J. Avis, M. Bloomer, G. Esland, D. Gleeson and P. Hodkinson (eds) *Knowledge and Nationhood*, London: Cassell.

Evans, J. (1985) *Teaching in Transition: The Challenge of Mixed Ability Grouping*, Milton Keynes: Open University Press.

Evans, J. (1990) 'Defining a subject: the rise and rise of the new PE?', *British Journal of Sociology of Education*, 11(2): 155–71.

Evans, J. and Davies, B. (2005) 'Social class and physical education', in D. Kirk and K. Hardman (eds) *Handbook of Research in Physical Education*, London: Sage.

Firestone, W.A., Fitz, J. and Broadfoot, P. (2000) 'Power, learning and legitimisation: assessment implementation across levels in the US and the UK', *American Educational Research Journal*, 36(2): 759–93.

Fitz, J. and Beers, B. (2002) 'Educational management organisations and the privatisation of education in the US and the UK', *Comparative Education*, 38(2): 137–54.

Fitz, J., Firestone, W.A. and Fairman, J. (2000) 'Local leaders: leadership in school and local educational authorities', in K. Riley and K.S. Louis (eds) *Leadership for Change: International Perspectives in Relational Leadership*, London: RoutledgeFalmer.

Fitz, J., Gorard, S. and Taylor, C. (2002a) 'School admissions after the School Standards and Framework Act: bringing the LEAs back in?', *Oxford Review of Education*, 28(2): 373–93.

Fitz, J., Halpin D. and Power, S. (1993) *Education in the Market Place*, London: Kogan Page.

Fitz, J., Halpin, D. and Power, S. (1997) 'Between a rock and a hard place: diversity, institutional identity and grant-maintained schools', *Oxford Review of Education*, 23(1): 17–30.

Fitz, J., Taylor, C., Gorard, S. and White, P. (2002b) 'LEAs and markets: four case studies', *Research Papers in Education*, 17(2): 1–22.

Floud, J. (1962) 'The sociology of education', in A.T. Welford, M. Argyle, D.V. Glass and J.N. Morris (eds) *Society: Problems and Methods of Study*, London: Routledge and Kegan Paul.

Floud, J. and Halsey, A.H. (1961) 'Social class, intelligence tests and selection for secondary schools', in A.H. Halsey, J. Floud and C. Arnold Anderson (eds) *Education, Economy and Society: A Reader in the Sociology of Education*, New York: The Free Press of Glencoe.

Floud, J., Halsey, A.H. and Martin, F.M. (1956) *Social Class and Educational Opportunity*, London: Heinemann.

Floud, J., Halsey A.H. and Martin, F.M. (1956) 'Social class and educational opportunity', in H. Silver (ed.) (1973) *Equal Opportunity in Education: A Reader in Social Class and Educational Opportunity*, London: Methuen.

Ford, J. (1969) *Social Class and the Comprehensive School*, London: Routledge and Kegan Paul.

Fuller, M. (1997) 'Equality and "race", Unit 4, Block 5, Equality and Education', *Exploring Educational Issues*, E 208 Education: a second level course, Milton Keynes: Open University.

Furlong, J. (2001) 'Reforming, teacher education, reforming teachers; accountability professionalism and competence', in R. Phillips and J. Furlong (eds) *Education, Reform and the State: Twenty-five years of Politics, Policy and Practice*, London: RoutledgeFalmer.

Galindo-Rueda, F. and Vignoles, A. (2003) *Class Ridden or Meritocratic? An Economic Analysis of Recent Changes in Britain*, London: Centre for Performance, London School of Economics and Political Science, downloaded from http://www.cee.lse.ac.uk.

Galton, M.J. (1998) *Reliving the ORACLE Experience: Back to Basics or Back to the Future?*, Warwick: Centre for Research in Elementary and Primary Education.

Galton, M.J. (1999) *Inside the Primary Classroom: Twenty Years on*, London: Routledge.

Galton, M.J., Simon, B. and Croll, P. (1980) *Inside the Primary School*, London: Routledge and Kegan Paul.

Gamoran, A. (1987) 'Organisation, induction and the effects of ability grouping: comment on Slavin's "best evidence thesis"', *Review of Educational Research*, 57(3): 341–5.

Gardiner, J. (1997) 'New teachers to be tested on English competence', *Times Educational Supplement*, 14 February: 1.

Garner, R. (2001) 'Inquiry urged into faith schools plan', *Independent*, 6 November, downloaded from http://www.independent.co.uk.

Gerwirtz, S. (1999) 'Education action zones: emblems of the third way?', in H. Dean and R. Woods (eds) *Social Policy Review 11*, Luton: Social Policy Association.

Gewirtz, S., Ball, S.J. and Bowe, R. (1995) *Markets, Choice and Equity in Education*, Buckingham: Open University Press.

Gillborn, D. and Youdell, D. (1999) *Rationing Education: Policy, Practice, Reform, and Equity*, Buckingham: Open University Press.

Gipps, C., Brown, M., McCallum, B. and McAlister, S. (1995) *Intuition or Evidence? Teachers and National Assessment of seven-year-olds*. Buckingham: Open University Press.

Glass, D.V. (ed.) (1954) *Social Mobility in Britain*, London: Routledge and Kegan Paul.

Glatter, R., Woods, P.A. and Bagley, C. (1997) *Choice of Diversity in Schooling*, London: Routledge.

Gleeson, D. (1989) *The Paradox of Training*, London: Methuen.

Glennerster, H. (1992) *Paying for Welfare: The 1990s*, 2nd rev. edn, New York and London: Harvester Wheatsheaf.

Goldthorpe, J. (2003) 'The myth of education-based meritocracy', *New Economy*, London: IPPR.

Goldthorpe, J., Llewellyn, C. and Payne, C. (1980) *Social Mobility and Class Structure in Modern Britain*, Oxford: Clarendon Press.

Gorard, S. (2000) *Education and Social Justice*, Cardiff: University of Wales Press.

Gorard, S. and Fitz, J. (2000) 'Investigating the determinants of segregation between schools', *Research Papers in Education*, 15(2): 115–32.

Gorard, S. and Rees, G. (2002) *Creating a Learning Society?: Learning Careers and Policies for Lifelong Learning*, Bristol: Policy Press.

Gorard, S. and Taylor, C. (2001) 'Specialist schools in England: track record and future prospect', *School Leadership and Management*, 21(4): 365–81.

Gorard, S., Taylor, C. and Fitz, J. (2003) *Schools, Markets and Choice Policies*, London: RoutledgeFalmer.

Gosden P. (1976) *Education in the Second World War: A Study in Policy and Administration*, London: Methuen.

Gould, S.J. (1981) *The Mismeasure of Man*, New York: W.W. Norton.

Gray, J.L. and Moshinsky, J. (1938) 'Ability and opportunity in English education', in H. Silver (ed.) (1973) *Equal Opportunity in Education: A Reader in Social Class and Educational Opportunity*, London: Methuen.

Gray, J., McPherson, A. and Raffe, D. (1983) *Reconstructions of Secondary Education: Theory, Myth and Practice since the War*, London: Routledge and Kegan Paul.

Grubb, N.W. and Finkelstein, N. (2000) 'Making sense of education and training markets: lessons from England', *American Educational Research Journal*, 37(3): 601–31.

Halliday, M.A.K. (1978) *Language as a Social Semiotic: The Social Interpretation of Language and Meaning*, London: Edward Arnold.

Halpin, D., Fitz, J. and Power, S. (1997) 'In the grip of the past? Tradition, traditionalism and contemporary schooling', *International Studies in Sociology of Education*, 7(1). 3–20.

Halpin. D., Nixon, J., Ranson, S. and Seddon, T. (eds) (2004) 'Renewing education for civic society', *London Review of Education*, Special Edition, 2(3).

Halsey, A.H. (ed.) (1972) *Trends in British Society Since 1900: A Guide to the Changing Social Structure of Britain*, London: Macmillan.

Halsey, A.H., Floud, J. and Anderson, C.A. (eds) (1961) *Education, Economy and Society*, New York: Free Press of Glencoe.

Halsey, A.H., Heath, A.F. and Ridge, J.M. (1980) *Origins and Destinations: Family, Class and Education in Modern Britain*, Oxford: Oxford University Press.

Hargreaves, D. (1967) *Social Relations in a Secondary School*, London: Routledge and Kegan Paul.

Hargreaves, D. (1996) 'Diversity and choice in school education: a modified libertarian approach', *Oxford Review of Education*, 22(2): 131–41.

Hasan, R. (2001) 'The ontogenesis of decontextualised language, in A. Morais, I. Neves, B. Davies and H. Daniels (eds) *Towards a Sociology of Pedagogy: The Contribution of Basil Bernstein to Research*, New York: Peter Lang.

Hasan, R. (2004) 'The concept of semiotic mediation: perspectives from Bernstein's sociology', in J. Muller, B. Davies and A. Morais (eds) *Reading Bernstein, Researching Bernstein*, London: RoutledgeFalmer.

Hatcher, R. (1998) 'Profiting from schools: business and education action zones', *Education and Social Justice*, 1(1): 9–16.

Hattersley, R. (2002) 'Selection returns by stealth', *The Guardian*, 25 February: 16.

Heath, A. (2000) 'The political arithmetic tradition in the sociology of education', *Oxford Review of Education*, 26(3): 313–31.

Her Majesty's Inspectorate (HMI) (1978) *Primary Education: A Survey by HMI Inspectors of Schools*, London: HMSO.

Her Majesty's Inspectorate (HMI) (1979) *Aspects of Secondary Education in England: A Survey by HMI Inspectors of Schools* London: HMSO.

Himmelweit, H. (1954) 'Social status and secondary education since the 1944 Act: some data for London', in H. Silver (ed.) (1973) *Equal Opportunity in Education: A Reader in Social Class and Educational Opportunity*, London: Methuen.

Hodgson, A. and Spours, K. (1999) *New Labour's Educational Agenda: Issues and Policies for Education and Training from 14+*, London: Kogan Page.

Hogben, L. (1938) *Political Arithmetic: A Symposium of Population Studies*, London: Allen and Unwin.

Holland, J. (1997) *Exploring Educational Issues. Block 5, Equality and Education; Unit 3, The Gender Agenda in Education*, Milton Keynes: Open Univerity Press.

Ireson, J. and Hallam, S. (2001) *Ability Grouping in Education*, London: Paul Chapman.

Ireson, J., Hallam, S. and Hurley, C. (2002) 'Ability grouping in secondary school: effects on GCSE attainment in English, mathematics and science', Paper presented to the British Educational Research Association, 28th Annual Conference, University of Exeter, September.

Jackson, B. (1970) *Streaming: An Education System in Miniature*, London: Routledge and Kegan Paul.

Jackson, B. and Marsden, B. (1966) *Education and the Working Class: Some General Themes Raised by a Study of 88 Working-class Children in a Northern Industrial City*, Harmondsworth: Penguin.

James, C. (1968) *Young Lives at Stake: A Reappraisal of Secondary Schools*, London: Collins.

Jeffrey, R. (2002) 'Performativity and primary teacher relations', *Journal of Education Policy*, 17(5): 531–46.

Jephcote, M. and Huddlestone, P. (2001) 'Further education: a suitable case for treatment?', in R. Phillips and J. Furlong (eds) *Education, Reform and the State: Twenty-five Years of Politics, Policy and Practice*, London: RoutledgeFalmer.

Jones, G.E. (1990) *Which Nations's Schools?: Direction and Devolution in Welsh Education in the Twentieth Century*, Cardiff: University of Wales Press.

Jones, G.E. (1997) *The Education of a Nation*, Cardiff: University of Wales Press.

Jones, K. (2003) *Education in Britain: 1944 to the Present*, Cambridge: Polity Press.

Jordan, B. (1985) *The State: Authority and Autonomy*, Blackwell: Oxford.

Jowett, S. (1995) *Allocating Secondary School Places*, Slough: National Foundation for Educational Research (NFER).

Kerckhoff, A., Fogelman, K., Crook, D. and Reeder, D. (1996) *Going Comprehensive in England and Wales: A Study of Uneven Change*, London: Woburn Press.

Knight, C. (1990) *The Making of Tory Education Policy in Post-War Britain*, London: Falmer Press.

Kogan, M. (1971) *The Politics of Education: Edward Boyle and Anthony Crosland in Conversation with Maurice Kogan*, Harmondsworth: Penguin.

Kogan, M. (1975) *Educational Policy-making*, London: Allen and Unwin.

Kogan, M. (2002) 'The subordination of local government and the compliant society', *Oxford Review of Education*, 28(2–3): 321–42.

Labour Party, The (1997) *New Labour: Because Britain Deserves Better*, 1997 Election Manifesto.

Labov, W. (1972) The logic of non-standard English, in P.P. Giglioli (ed.) *Language and Social Context*, Harmondsworth: Penguin.

Lacey, C. (1970) *Hightown Grammar*, Manchester: Manchester University Press.

Lane, J.-E. (1993) *The Public Sector, Concepts, Models and Approaches*, London: Sage.

Lauder, H., Hughes, D., Watson, S., Waslander, S., Thrupp, M., Strathdee, R., Simiyu, I., Dupuis, A., McGlinn, J. and Hamlin, J. (1999) *Trading in Futures: Why Markets in Education Don't Work*, Buckingham: Open University Press.

Lawson, J. and Silver, H. (1973) *A Social History of Education in England*, London: Methuen.

Levin, B. (2001) *Reforming Education: From Origins to Outcomes*, London: RoutledgeFalmer.

Lindsay, K. (1926) *Social Progress and Educational Waste: Being a Study of the 'Free Place' Scholarship System*, London: Routledge.

Mackinnon, D., Statham, J. and Hales, M. (1996) *Education in the UK: Facts and Figures*, London: Hodder and Stoughton, in association with the Open University.

Maclure, S. (1989) *Education Re-formed: A Guide to the Education Reform Act*, London: Hodder and Stoughton.

Maclure, S. (2000) *The Inspectors' Calling: HMI and the Shaping of Educational Policy 1945–1992*, London: Hodder and Stoughton.

Marsh, L.G. (1970) *Alongside the Child in the Primary School*, London: Black.

Marsh, L.G. (1973) *Becoming a Teacher*, London: A&C Black.

Marshall, G., Swift, A. and Roberts, S. (1997) *Against All Odds: Social Class and Social Justice in Industrial Societies*, Oxford: Clarendon Press.

Maton, K. (2004) 'The wrong kind of knower: education, expansion and the epistemic device', in J. Muller, B. Davies and A. Morais (eds) *Reading Bernstein, Researching Bernstein*, London: RoutledgeFalmer.

Ministry of Education (1947) *The New Secondary Education*, London: HMSO.

Ministry of Education, Consultative Committee on Secondary Education (1938) *Report of the Consultative Committee on Secondary Education with Special Reference to Grammar Schools and Technical High Schools, Spens Report*, London: HMSO.

Morais, A., Neves, I,. Davies, B. and Daniels, H. (eds) (2001) *Towards a Sociology of Pedagogy: The Contribution of Basil Bernstein to Research*, New York: Peter Lang.

Morais, A., Neves, I. and Pires, D. (2004) 'The *what* and the *how* of teaching and learning. Going deeper into sociological analysis and intervention', in J. Muller, B. Davies and A. Morais (eds) *Reading Bernstein, Researching Bernstein*, London: RoutledgeFalmer.

Morris, E. (2001) 'We need your help to make the difference', *Educational Review*, 15(1): 2–7.

Muller, J. (2000) *Reclaiming Knowledge: Social Theory, Curriculum and Education Policy*, London: RoutledgeFalmer.

Muller, J. (2004) 'Introduction: the possibilities of Basil Bernstein', in J. Muller, B. Davies and A. Morais (eds) *Reading Bernstein, Researching Bernstein*, London: RoutledgeFalmer.

Muller, J., Davies, B. and Morais, A. (eds) (2004) *Reading Bernstein, Researching Bernstein*, London: RoutledgeFalmer.

Nash, R. (1973) *Classrooms Observed*, London: Routledge and Kegan Paul.

Neves, I., Morais, A. and Afonso, M. (2004) 'Teacher training contexts: study of specific sociological characteristics', in J. Muller, B. Davies and A. Morais (eds) *Reading Bernstein, Researching Bernstein*, London: RoutledgeFalmer.

Norwood Report (1943) *Report of the Committee of the Secondary Schools Examination Council on Curriculum and Examinations in Secondary Schools*, London: HMSO.

OFSTED (2001) *Specialist Schools: An Evaluation of Progress*, London: OFSTED.

O'Keeffe, D. and Stoll, P. (eds) (1995) *Issues in School Attendance and Truancy: Understanding and Managing the Problem*, London: Pitman.

Paterson, L. (2003) 'The three educational ideologies of the British Labour Party, 1997–2001', *Oxford Review of Education*, 29(2): 165–86.

Pedley, R. (1974) *The Comprehensive School*, Harmondsworth: Penguin.

Penney, D. (2004) 'Policy tensions being played out in practice: the specialist schools initiative in England', *Journal for Critical Education Policy Studies*, 2(1), downloaded from http://www.jceps.com.

Penney, D. and Evans, J. (1999) *Politics, Policy and Practice in Physical Education*, London: E & FN Spon.

Phillips, R. (2001) 'Education, the state and the politics of reform: the historical context, 1876–2001', in R. Phillips and J. Furlong (eds) *Education, Reform and the State: Twenty-five Years of Politics, Policy and Practice*, London: RoutledgeFalmer.

Phillips, R. and Furlong, J. (2001) *Education, Reform and the State: Twenty-five Years of Policy, Politics and Practice*, London: RoutledgeFalmer.

Pollard, A. (1990) 'Toward a sociology of learning in primary schools', *British Journal of Sociology of Education*, 11(2): 242–56.

Pollard, A., Broadfoot, P., Croll, P., Osbourne, M. and Abbott, D. (1994) *Changing English Primary Schools?* London: Cassell.

Power, S. and Whitty, G. (1999) 'New Labour's education policy: first, second or third way?', *Journal of Education Policy*, 14(5): 535–46.

Power, S., Edwards, T., Whitty, G. and Wigfall, V. (2003) *Education and the Middle Class*, Buckingham: Open University Press.

Prandy, K., Lambert, P. and Bottero, W. (2003) 'By slow degrees: two centuries of social reproduction and mobility in Britain', unpublished paper, Cardiff University, School of Social Sciences.

Prandy, K., Unt, M. and Lambert, K. (2004) 'Not by degrees: education and social reproduction in twentieth-century Britain', unpublished paper, Cardiff University, School of Social Sciences.

Rees, G. and Stroud, D. (2001) 'Creating a mass system of HE: participation, the economy and citizenship', in R. Philips and J. Furlong (eds) (2001) *Education, Reform and the State: Twenty-five Years of Politics, Policy and Practice*, London: RoutledgeFalmer.

Reynolds, D. and Sullivan, L. (1987) *The Comprehensive Experiment*, London: Falmer Press.

Rhodes, R.A.W. (1997) *Understanding Governance: Policy Networks, Governance, Reflexivity and Accountability*, Buckingham: Open University Press.

Riley, K.A. and Louis, K.S. (2000) *Leadership: For Change and Social Reform*, London: RoutledgeFalmer.

Rist, R. (1970) 'Student social class and teacher expectations: the self-fulfilling prophecy in ghetto education', *Harvard Educational Review*, 40(3): 411–51.

Rogers, R. (1984) *Crowther to Warnock: How Fourteen Reports Tried to Change Children's Lives*, 2nd edn, London: Heinemann Educational Books.

Rosen, H. (1974) 'Language and class', in D. Holly (ed.) *Education and Domination*, London: Hutchinson (Arrow).

Rothstein, B. and Steinmo, S. (2002) *Restructuring the Welfare State: Political Institutions and Policy Change*, Basingstoke: Palgrave Macmillan.

Rudd, P., Rickinson, M., Blenkinsop, S., McMeeking, S., Taylor, M. and Phillips, N. (2002) *Long-Term External Evaluation of the Beacon Schools Initiative 2001–2002*, Slough: National Foundation for Educational Research (NFER).

Sadovnik, A. (ed.) (1995) *Basil Bernstein: Consensus and Controversy*, Norwood, NJ: Ablex.

Salisbury, J. and Riddell, S. (2000) *Gender, Policy and Educational Change: Shifting Agendas in the UK and Europe*, London: Routledge.

Salter, B. and Tapper, T. (1981) *Education, Politics and the State: The Theory and Practice of Educational Change*, London: Grant McIntyre.

Sanderson, M. (1985) *Educational Opportunity and Social Change in England*, London: Faber and Faber.

Sanderson, M. (1994) *The Missing Stratum: Technical School Education in England 1900–1990*, London: Athlone Press.

Saunders, P. (1981) *Social Theory and the Urban Question*, London: Hutchinson.

Saunders, P. (1996) *Unequal but Fair? A Study of Class Barriers in Britain*, London: Institute of Economic Affairs, Health and Welfare Unit.

Selwyn, N. and Fitz, J. (2001) 'The National Grid for Learning: a case study of education policy making under New Labour', *Journal of Education Policy*, 16(2): 127–47.

Sharp, R. and Green, A. (1975) *Education and Social Control*, London: Routledge and Kegan Paul.

Sharpe, L.J. (ed.) (1993) *The Rise of Meso Government in Europe*, London: Sage.

Shaw, B. (1983) *Comprehensive Schooling: The Impossible Dream?*, Oxford: Basil Blackwell.

Shulman, L. (2004) *The Wisdom of Practice: Essays on Teaching, Learning and Learning to Teach*, edited by S.M. Wilson, San Francisco: Jossey-Bass.

Silver, H. (ed.) (1973) *Equal Opportunity in Education: A Reader in Social Class and Educational Opportunity*, London: Methuen.

Simon, B. (1953) *Intelligence Testing and the Comprehensive School*, London: Lawrence and Wishart.

Simon, B. (1971) *Intelligence, Psychology and Education: A Marxist Critique*, London: Lawrence and Wishart.

Simon, B. and Rubenstein, D. (1969) *The Evolution of the Comprehensive School*, London: Routledge and Kegan Paul.

Simon, D.S. (1948) *Three Schools or One? Secondary Education in England, Scotland and the USA*, London: Frederick Muller.

Singh, P. (2002) 'Pedagogising knowledge: Bernstein's theory of the pedagogic device', *British Journal of Sociology of Education*, 23(4): 571–82.

Skocpol, T. (1992) *Protecting Soldiers and Mothers. The Political Origins of Social Policy in the United States*, Cambridge, MA: Belknap Press.

Smetheram, C. (2004) *First Class Women in the World of Work: Employability and Labour Market Orientations*, Working Paper No. 45, Cardiff, Cardiff School of Social Sciences.

Statham, J., Mackinnon, D. and Cathcart, H. (1989) *The Education Fact File: A Handbook of Educational Information in the UK*, London: Hodder and Stoughton.

Steedman, J. (1983a) *Progress in Secondary Schools*, London: National Children's Bureau.

Steedman, J. (1983b) *Examination Results in Selective and Non-Selective Schools*, London: National Children's Bureau.

Steinmo, S., Thelen, K. and Longstreth, F. (eds) (1992) *Structuring Politics: Historical Institutionalism In Comparative Analysis*, Cambridge: Cambridge University Press.

Tapper, T. and Salter, B. (1978) *Education and the Political Order: Changing Patterns of Class Control*, London: Macmillan.

Tawney, R.H. (ed.) (1922) *Secondary Education for All: A Policy for Labour*, London: Allen and Unwin.

Taylor, C. (2001a) 'The geography of choice and diversity in the "new" secondary education market of England', *Area*, 33(4): 368–81.

Taylor, C. (2001b) 'Hierarchies and "local" markets: the geography of the "lived" market place in secondary education provision', *Journal of Education Policy*, 16(3): 197–214.

Taylor, C. (2002) *Geography of the 'New' Education Market*, Aldershot: Ashgate.

Taylor, C. and Gorard, S. (2001) 'The role of residence in segregation: placing the impact of parental choice in perspective', *Environment and Planning A*, 33(10): 1829–52.

Taylor, C., Gorard, S. and Fitz, J. (2002) 'Market frustration; admission appeals in the UK education market', *Educational Management and Administration*, 30(3): 243–60.

Taylor, C., Gorard, S. and Fitz, J. (2003) 'The modifiable areal unit problem: segregation between schools and levels of analysis', *International Journal of Social Research Methodology*, 16(1): 41–60.

Taylor, S., Rizvi, F., Lingard, B. and Henry, M. (1997) *Educational Policy and the Politics of Change*, London: Routledge.

Taylor, W. (1963) *The Secondary Modern School*, London: Faber and Faber.

Taylor-Gooby, P. (1991) *Social Change, Welfare and Social Science*, New York and London: Harvester Wheatsheaf.

Thomas, H. (1990) *Education Costs and Performance: A Cost Effectiveness Analysis*, London: Cassell.

Thornton, K. (2001) 'Specialists spark "two-tier" fears', *Times Educational Supplement*, 8 June: 34.

Tomlinson, S. (2001) *Education in Post-welfare Society*, Buckingham: Open University Press.

Tomlinson, S. (2004) 'Comprehensive success and bog-standard government', Third Caroline Benn Memorial Lecture, downloaded from http://www.socialisteducation. org.uk/CB3.htm.

Tooley, J. (2000) *Reclaiming Education*, London: Cassell.

Toynbee, P. (2001) 'Keep God out of class', *The Guardian*, 9 November, downloaded from http//www.education.guardian.co.uk 20/3/02.

Trowler, P. (1998) *Education Policy: A Policy Sociology Approach*, Eastbourne: Gildredge Press.

Trowler, P. (2003) *Education Policy*, London: Routledge.

Twine, F. (1994) *Citizenship and Social Rights*, London: Sage.

Tyler, W. (2004) 'Silent, invisible, total: pedagogic discourse and the age of information', in J. Muller, B. Davies and A. Morais (eds) *Reading Bernstein, Researching Bernstein*, London: RoutledgeFalmer.

Vernon, P. (1952) *Secondary School Selection: A British Psychological Society Investigation*, London: Methuen.

Vygotsky, L.S. (1978) *Mind and Society: The Development of Higher Psychological Processes*, edited by M. Cole, V. John-Steiner, S. Scribner and E. Souberman, Cambridge, MA: Harvard University Press.

Wall, A. and Owen, B. (1999) *Health Policy, Health Care and the NHS*, Eastbourne: Gildredge Press.

Ward, L. (2004) ' "Oxford could go private in 15 years", says head of Trinity College', *The Guardian*, Wednesday, 6 October: 3.

Weaver, T. (1986) 'The policy makers: local and central government', Module 2, E333, *Policy Making in Education*, Milton Keynes: The Open University.

Webster, D. and Parsons, K. (1999) 'Labour Party policy on educational selection 1996–98: a sociological analysis', *Journal of Education Policy*, 14(5): 547–59.

Welsh Assembly Government (2002) *Statistical Bulletin, Assessment and Examination Performance in Wales: Comparison with England and its Regions*, 21 May: 1–9.

West, A. and Hind, A. (2003) *Secondary School Admissions in England: Exploring the Extent of Overt and Covert Selection*, London: Research and Information on State Education Trust.

West, A., Noden, P., Pennel, H. and Travers, T. (2000) *Examining the Impact of the Specialist Schools Programme*, Research Report RR196, London: DfEE.

White, J. (1975) 'The end of the compulsory curriculum', in *The Curriculum: The Doris Lee Lectures*, Studies in Education, new series, 2, London: Institute of Education.

White, P., Gorard, S., Fitz, J. and Taylor, C. (2001) 'Regional and local differences in admission arrangements for schools', *Oxford Review of Education*, 27(3): 317–37.

Whitty, G. (1995) 'Education policy and the sociology of education', *International Studies in Sociology of Education*, 7(2): 121–35.

Whitty, G., Edwards, T. and Gewirtz, S. (1993) *Specialisation and Choice in Urban Education: The City Technology Colleges Experiment*, London: Routledge.

Whitty, G., Power, S. and Halpin, D. (1998) *Devolution and Choice in Education: The School, the State and the Market*, Buckingham and Philadelphia, PA: Open University Press.

Wiliam, D. and Bartholomew, H. (2004) 'Ability grouping and student progress', *British Educational Research Journal*, 30(2): 278–92.

Willis, P. (2002) 'Increased tension', *The Guardian*, 4 February, downloaded from http://www.education.guardian.co.uk.

Witte, J. (1990) 'Introduction', in J.W. Clune and J. Witte (eds) *Choice and Control in American Education, Volume 1: The Theory of Choice and Control in Education*, London: Falmer Press.

Woods, P., Bagley, C. and Glatter, R. (1997) *School, Choice and Competition: Markets in the Public Interest*, London and New York: Routledge.

Wright, C., Weekes, D. and McGlaughlin, A. (2000) *'Race', Class and Gender and Exclusion from School*, London: Falmer Press.

Yeomans, D., Higham, J. and Sharp, P. (2000) *The Impact of the Specialist Schools Programme: Case Studies*, Research Report RR197, London: DfEE.

Young, M.F.D. (1971) 'An approach to the study of curricula as socially organised knowledge', in M.F.D. Young (ed.) *Knowledge and Control: New Directions for the Sociology of Education*, London: Collier-Macmillan.

Index